MW00639534

COUNTERING CHINA'S GREAT GAME

COUNTERING CHINA'S GREAT GAME

A Strategy for American Dominance

MICHAEL SOBOLIK

Naval Institute Press
Annapolis, Maryland

Naval Institute Press
291 Wood Road
Annapolis, MD 21402

Library of Congress Cataloging-in-Publication Data

Names: Sobolik, Michael, author.
Title: Countering China's great game : a strategy for American dominance /
  Michael Sobolik.
Description: First printing. | Annapolis, Maryland : Naval Institute Press,
  [2024] | Includes bibliographical references and index.
Identifiers: LCCN 2023054218 (print) | LCCN 2023054219 (ebook) | ISBN
  9781682479506 (hardback) | ISBN 9781682479513 (ebook)
Subjects: LCSH: United States—Foreign relations—China. | China—Foreign
  relations—United States. | China—Strategic aspects. | Yi dai yi lu
  (Initiative : China) | Geopolitics—China. | China—Foreign
  relations—21st century. | United States—Foreign relations—21st
  century. | BISAC: HISTORY / Asia / China | POLITICAL SCIENCE /
  World / Asian
Classification: LCC E183.8.C5 S59 2024 (print) | LCC E183.8.C5 (ebook) |
  DDC 327.73051—dc23/eng/20231229
LC record available at https://lccn.loc.gov/2023054218
LC ebook record available at https://lccn.loc.gov/2023054219

♾ Print editions meet the requirements of ANSI/NISO z39.48–1992 (Per-
manence of Paper).
Printed in the United States of America.

32 31 30 29 28 27 26 25 24   9 8 7 6 5 4 3 2 1
First printing

For Chelsea and Dev, who always hold my heart

CONTENTS

MAPS

FOREWORD

AS A POLICY STAFFER working for a U.S. senator, Michael Sobolik sat down in the fall of 2017 for what would turn out to be "the most peculiar meeting I ever took." Sobolik had accepted what he thought would be an unremarkable appointment with a Singaporean businessman he was meeting for the first time. It was common courtesy for Capitol Hill staffers to accept requests for meetings by all sorts of visitors to Washington—constituents, activists, businesspeople.

Soon after the meeting started, however, "it became abundantly clear that I was engaging in unofficial negotiations with Chinese officials," Sobolik recounts in this book. The Singaporean businessman had brought some men with him who Sobolik believes were if not officials from Beijing, then people closely aligned with its interests.

The delegation urged Sobolik to convince his boss, Senator Ted Cruz of Texas, to abandon a legislative proposal to rename a street in Washington, D.C. And not just any street: Cruz's bill, if voted into law, would rename the road in front of China's embassy as "Liu Xiaobo Plaza," in honor of a democracy activist who had recently died in police custody in Beijing. Liu was only the second Nobel Peace Prize laureate ever to die as a political prisoner. (The first was German journalist Carl von Ossietzky, who perished in the custody of the Nazis in 1938.)

The strangers went so far as to suggest to Sobolik that Liu's widow, Liu Xia, might never be allowed to leave China unless Senator Cruz backed down and withdrew his bill. That sounded to Sobolik like a threat—the sort of cynical dilemma the Chinese Communist Party (CCP) is expert at manufacturing when it wants to exert pressure. Sobolik kept his nerve and stood his ground. The strangers left empty-handed. Senator Cruz persisted in advocating for his legislation, and Chinese diplomats and their lickspittles remained preoccupied with trying to counter it.

While the bill never did become law (other U.S. senators blocked it), the episode and its two central lessons stayed with Sobolik. First, nothing strikes a nerve with China's Communist rulers quite like spotlighting their systemic abuse of human rights. Second, imposing costs on Beijing for its disregard of basic rights isn't only morally correct: it's also the basis for sound strategic policymaking. These insights form the heart of *Countering China's Great Game*.

Only four decades ago, in the final years of the last Cold War, these lessons were applied by the United States with decisive results. President Ronald Reagan rejected his predecessors' policy of détente with the Soviet Union and replaced it with a policy of *candor*.

Candor was Reagan's idea that democracies are safest when they speak honestly and publicly about their adversaries and the nature of their regimes. This took some getting used to. When Reagan was preparing to give a speech in Berlin in 1987, several of his staff tried desperately to get him to remove a phrase they found embarrassing and needlessly provocative. Luckily, President Reagan went with his gut and delivered the most famous line of his presidency: "Mr. Gorbachev, tear down this wall."

Elite opinion argued that calling out the Soviet Union on its rights abuses, as Reagan so often did, was confrontational and dangerous. The Soviet Communists back then, like Chinese Communists today, used such thinking against us. By portraying truth-telling as an act of belligerence, autocrats try to badger democracies into silence—and often succeed. "This is the first and most important defeat free nations can ever suffer," President Reagan told his British hosts in a speech at Guildhall in 1988. "When free peoples cease telling the truth about and to their adversaries, they cease telling the truth to themselves." Public candor, Reagan knew, actually promotes peace by reducing the space for strategic miscalculation.

It also wrings Communist Party propaganda of its potency. CCP propaganda consistently tells foreign audiences two big lies: "We own the future, so make your adjustments now." And: "We're not so different from democratic governments, so there's nothing to worry about."

In the pages that follow, Sobolik exposes the con at the heart of those assertions. He shows how many of Beijing's perceived strengths are actually critical vulnerabilities. Far from owning the future, the CCP is making policy misjudgments that may make it one of the Middle Kingdom's shorter-lived dynasties. Far from being a "normal" government, the CCP is engaging in crimes against humanity, most notably through its genocide of minority populations in Xinjiang.

Sobolik offers some bold policy and legal remedies designed to point a hot spotlight on these atrocities and to make them economically costly for the CCP. "It is not incumbent on representative democracies like the United States to make allowances for the CCP's pathologies," Sobolik advises. The United States, he reminds us, needs to dispense with timid and self-doubting policies and rhetoric that are devoid of the recognition that we are in a contest of values. Reagan would recognize the imperative underscored by Sobolik. So, too, hopefully, will a new generation of readers, voters, and leaders.

MATT POTTINGER

Chairman of the China Program at the Foundation for Defense of Democracies, former U.S. Deputy National Security Adviser

ACKNOWLEDGMENTS

NOTHING OF VALUE is accomplished alone. My entire life is a testament to this truth, and this project is no exception. Truthfully, I was unprepared for the intellectual and professional demands of writing a book. I was equally unprepared for the level of encouragement and support I received along the way from bosses, mentors, colleagues, and family.

This book would never have materialized without the personal support of Herman Pirchner Jr. and the institutional backing of the American Foreign Policy Council (AFPC). When I left Capitol Hill in the summer of 2019, my confidence exceeded my knowledge. Even so, Herman took a chance on me. I owe every bit of success at AFPC to Herman's patience and encouragement. His foreign policy sagacity is outmatched only by his care for his employees.

For the financial backing for this book, I owe a debt of gratitude to the Diana Davis Spencer Foundation. To Diana Davis Spencer, Abby Moffat, Elizabeth Smiroldo, Christopher Burn, and the entire team: thank you for believing in this project.

I had the great fortune of working with the team at Naval Institute Press on this project. Thanks to Adam Kane and Pat Carlin for your professionalism and support. To my agent Ingrid Beck: thank you for finding the best possible home for this book.

The idea for *Countering China's Great Game* started in 2018, when I first encountered net assessments and competitive strategies at a multiday training seminar hosted by the American Academy for Strategic Education (AASE). To Aaron Friedberg, Jacqueline Deal, and Stephen Rosen: you have my utmost respect and admiration. Thank you for planting the seed that became this book.

My colleagues at AFPC offered support and wisdom that sustained me throughout this journey. To Ilan Berman: thanks for pushing me to write this book and for putting up with all my questions and knocks on your office door. To Rich Harrison: thanks for guiding me through the book-writing journey when I had no idea where I was going. To Annie Swingen: thanks for all the ways you supported my family, especially Dev, during this process. To Sydney Duckor and Rehna Sheth: you both embody service and leadership, and AFPC is blessed for it. Special thanks go to AFPC's all-star interns who put up with countless research requests along the way: Marian Balceiro, Alex Chavez, Esteban Espinoza, Jordan Ferree, Kyra Gustavsen, Alexandra Jaramillo, Tiffany Kim, Blake Kravitz, Jacoby Ramsey, Kyle Sajoyan, and Gracia Watson.

Beyond AFPC, a host of China hands, journalists, and current and former government officials lent their time and expertise to refining my ideas and critiquing my arguments. Any wisdom readers glean from these pages is due to their patient examination and review. To Dan Blumenthal, Ian Easton, Sophie Richardson, Brent Sadler, Michael Schuman, Nury Turkel, Larry Wortzel, and an anonymous reviewer: your insights were indispensable. Thank you.

During this time, Herman was kind enough to support my concept for a podcast focusing on great power competition.

These pages carry more than a few nuggets of wisdom gleaned from those conversations. To all the guests of *Great Power Podcast*: thanks for coming on the show.

While writing this book, I had the distinct honor of hosting AFPC-sponsored off-the-record dinners in Washington. The premise was simple: bring senior bipartisan congressional staff and senior administration officials together for private conversations about China. Set aside the 95 percent of disagreements for two hours and focus on the 5 percent Democrats and Republicans could cooperate on. No details from these gatherings appear in this book, but the leadership of officials and staffers across party lines provided untold inspiration. To those who have joined these meals: your willingness to set partisanship aside and break bread together gives me hope for our country's future.

I owe everything to the professors, teachers, and mentors who invested in my life and taught me how to think and communicate. Jasen Castillo: Your courses alone made graduate school two of the best years of my life. Thanks for pushing me to a higher level of analysis. Your words still ring in my head: "Always do the reading." Ben Freeman: Your summer term foreign policy class in 2010 was my first exposure to the topic. Your encouragement made me brave enough to go deeper. Dan Fredrick: I still remember the day and month you told me in 2009, "Go into law or politics." Thanks for seeing something in me and fanning it into flames. Gerri Colvin: You taught me that speaking well is more important than winning a high school debate tournament. At the time I didn't understand why, but now I think I get it. Connection, not conquest, is the goal.

To my parents, Mike and Liz: words fall short. Dad, I learned to listen to others because you always listened to me.

Mom, your laughter and love for life inspire me to take Washington (and myself) a little less seriously. Thank you for everything.

To Chelsea, my wife and best friend: Marrying you has brought more joy into my life than I ever knew was possible. Your professional accomplishments are surpassed only by your love for others and drive to speak for those who cannot speak for themselves. Thank you for supporting me throughout this entire process. All my love, all my life.

To our son, Dev: You are more loved than you could possibly know. Your mom and I are always proud of you—not for what you do, but for who you are.

A NOTE ON TERMS

CHINA'S NAME FOR its premier foreign policy project has remained unchanged for more than a decade: "一带一路," or "One Belt, One Road" (OBOR). Not long after announcing its plan to remake the world order, Beijing rebranded the project in its English-language publications to the more benign and inclusive-sounding "Belt and Road Initiative" (BRI). Both names describe the same project, but infer different meanings. "One Belt, One Road" is charged with ambition and makes an exclusivity claim that borders on the religious. The "Belt and Road Initiative" has the charisma of a faculty lounge presentation.

For better or worse, the broader policy community in the United States has widely accepted the BRI terminology. While OBOR is more accurate linguistically and strategically, I refrain from swimming upstream in these pages and adopt the revised acronym. To paraphrase Shakespeare, the BRI by any other name would be just as threatening.

INTRODUCTION

"**T**HIRTY DAYS.**" The answer was instant and emotionless but hung heavy in the air. The speaker was an official in Taiwan's Ministry of National Defense. A bipartisan delegation of staffers from the U.S. Congress had just asked how long Taiwan could hold off an invasion from the People's Republic of China (PRC) without America's support. I was a Senate aide at the time in 2016, and recall the silence that filled the room after the official's grim response.

Two years later, during a visit to the United States Indo-Pacific Command (USINDOPACOM) in Honolulu, Hawaii, I posed a similar question to senior officers at Pacific Air Forces (PACAF): "What's your Taiwan contingency? How prepared are you to engage if the PRC attacks Taiwan and the president orders you to respond?" Granted, it was an unclassified setting, and conversations of a sensitive nature can only go so far. But body language speaks volumes. For a few seconds, the PACAF advisers shifted in their chairs. Some chuckled. One of them finally responded, "We would need to withdraw our assets from the region in order to redeploy them."

I sat back, stunned. I still am. If Taiwan only has a month at best without America's help, we cannot afford to lose time. America needs to be prepared to fight and determined to win—and not only us, but our allies and partners as well. Reality, however, is rarely so simple.

The United States of America is a global power with military bases in every critical region of the world. In East Asia, the bulk of U.S. might emanates from Japan—specifically, Kadena Air Base on the island of Okinawa, merely 450 miles away from Taiwan. Its proximity to Taipei complicates military planning for the People's Liberation Army (PLA), the armed forces of the Chinese Communist Party (CCP)—but it also cuts the other way. U.S. forces and the people of Japan lie under the growing shadow of China's ballistic missiles, which number in the thousands. The survival and resiliency of America's forward-deployed troops and assets in the early hours of a war with Beijing are an open question. In recent years, this inescapable reality has complicated America's military planning with allies from Tokyo and Seoul to Manila and Bangkok—all of whom are equally vulnerable. No one wants to get caught in a war between the eagle and the dragon. The entire world has grown wealthy from China's economic rise, while many also enjoy the safety of America's military presence. Americans have also grown unconsciously accustomed to this arrangement in the form of low prices for consumer goods buttressed by globalized supply chains that often run through the PRC. After all, this is the promise of globalism: everyone wins if everybody cooperates.

We are no longer living in a world where we can have it all. It is a world marked by danger, conflict, and the threat of great power warfare. Truthfully, the world has always been this way. Americans are merely returning from a rare vacation from reality. To be sure, the U.S. military has been no stranger to combat over the past two decades. But as James Fallows, contributing writer to the *Atlantic*, has observed, a mere fraction of 1 percent of Americans served in Afghanistan and Iraq.[1] As more and more time passed since that fateful morning of September 11, 2001, life for Americans seemingly grew safe from foreign attack. Today, in 2024, that illusion is shattering, and the sooner the better. Vladimir Putin's invasion of Ukraine in February 2022 heralded the return of great power warfare on the doorstep of the North Atlantic Treaty Organization (NATO). The CCP's appetite for subsuming Taiwan could implicate America in a fight that would look less like Kabul or Fallujah and more like Normandy and Hiroshima.

Avoiding World War III will require more than winning the military balance. Denying Beijing a credible shot at taking Taiwan is necessary, but insufficient. Xi Jinping, the CCP's cold and calculating helmsman, may be willing to start a war, but he is clearly angling to achieve his objectives short of fighting. That is the sum of Beijing's foreign policy: creating favorable conditions for the return of Chinese imperialism and the decline of American power. Xi wants China to dominate the world. Accordingly, the CCP is bending information, trade, diplomacy, technology, and military might in service of that ambition. Xi's pet project, the Belt and Road Initiative (BRI), encapsulates this gambit to "win without fighting," as Sun Tzu wrote. It is the CCP's "great game" to shift the world's economic orientation away from America and toward the PRC, much like how imperial Britain and tsarist Russia maneuvered for control of Eurasia in the nineteenth century. In China's case, however, the objective exceeds a single continent. To the CCP, winning means exerting political dominance across the entire globe.

In many ways, Beijing has made great strides. Of the world's 195 countries, roughly 150 have signed BRI memoranda of understanding with the PRC (see map 1). Even so, Xi is running out of time to pull off his master plan, as China's demographics sour and its economic growth slows. In 2022, China's government reported a population decline, a trend the United Nations has forecasted to continue until at least 2100.[2] Corresponding economic woes are calling into question the long-accepted conventional wisdom that China will eventually surpass the United States economically.[3] Of course, these assumptions are just that. Whether the CCP's striving for greatness amounts to a sprint or a marathon, the party is not going anywhere, and neither is the BRI.

When I left Capitol Hill in 2019 to join the American Foreign Policy Council, a Washington, DC–based think tank, I asked numerous congressional China hands what help they needed the most: "What do you see as the biggest issue with the CCP that America needs to get right?" The consistent answer was the Belt and Road Initiative.

Many authors have written books about the BRI, primarily as an economic endeavor. My approach is complementary, but different. It is one thing to know how crime syndicates cook the books; it's another thing to understand why they cook them in the first place. These pages are dedicated to explaining why Xi Jinping and the CCP are seeking to change the world, what they hope to accomplish, and what Washington can do to head Beijing off at the pass before it's too late.

To be sure, the BRI of 2024 is not the BRI of 2019, let alone 2016, the approximate year when the project reached its zenith. Beijing is slimming down the Belt and Road and retooling its focus. This shift has led many pundits and scholars in Washington to downplay the project's ongoing importance. In late 2022, *Washington Post* columnist Fareed Zakaria called the BRI an "expensive and messy" dud.[4] In early 2023, *Foreign Policy* journalist Christina Lu characterized the BRI as "floundering" and "a shadow of its former self," a project that only continues because of its political importance to Xi Jinping.[5] These critiques misjudge the BRI's true purpose, but they also misunderstand the CCP's strategic intent. At its core, the BRI is not an economic venture. It is a geopolitical gambit. China's slowing economy is largely responsible for the reduced pace of BRI projects, true enough. But Xi's "project of the century" has entered its second phase: leveraging yesterday's investments for today's political and military ends. Xi Jinping is unlikely to nix the BRI because, for now, it is strengthening Beijing's strategic position from Southeast Asia and the Pacific islands to Africa and Latin America. The BRI is the apotheosis of the CCP's grand strategy. What America needs, then, is a blueprint to counter it.

This book is my effort to meet that need. More specifically, it is a plan to avoid war with the CCP not only by outgunning or outmaneuvering them but by outsmarting them. As such, it is an unapologetic proposal for prevailing against the CCP in a competition that is, unfortunately, zero-sum. There will be a winner and a loser in the twenty-first century. The goal of everything that follows is to ensure America's victory and the CCP's defeat.

Equally important, however, this book is not an unmitigated paean to American greatness. The United States is an exceptional nation, but it is also exceptionally bad at grand strategy. These pages are not only an exposition of Xi's designs but also a critique of the naive stories Washington elites have believed and the reactive policies they have embraced. Nothing is guaranteed or promised. If we are to win, Americans must compete shrewdly.

Chapter 1 begins here: exposing the lies we have believed about ourselves and China, and tracing their origins. Chapter 2 challenges Americans to reckon with the return of imperialism in our day and age and examines the roots of China's strategic culture going back thousands of years. Chapter 3 illuminates the impact of China's dynastic expansionism on its foreign policy today and reveals how the BRI is, at its heart, an imperial project. Chapter 4 examines Washington's strategy toward the CCP, exposes its deficiencies, and looks back to the first Cold War for inspiration to winning the second one today. Chapter 5 sketches out a plan to disrupt the BRI around the world, and chapter 6 traces those roots back to China and recommends policies to exploit the party's weaknesses at home. We will not prevail in this conflict by merely outcompeting our adversary. We must also take steps to frustrate Beijing's strategy.

Some may wonder how a small island like Taiwan could possibly implicate America in a third world war, or how Beijing-backed infrastructure projects across Eurasia could threaten Americans in Des Moines, Concord, or Columbia. We are, after all, separated from much of the world by the two largest oceans. America's isolated geography obscures how we stand in the way of the avarice and ambitions of despots and dictators. That reality, however, is abundantly clear to Xi Jinping. Immediately after seizing the reins of power in China, Xi compelled the party's senior echelon to study the strategic failures of the Soviet Union. The opening line of his propaganda film to CCP cadres minced no words: "The process of China's realization of the great undertaking of national rejuvenation must ultimately follow from testing and struggle against the system of American hegemony."[6]

America, by virtue of its power and ideology, stands athwart authoritarianism and imperialism, oftentimes without Americans realizing it. Whether we know it or not, we are once again living in a cold war. I still remember the day this reality mugged me in 2018, when the president of an internationally recognized cancer research center visited the Senate and warned me that the CCP was stealing advanced radiology research from their institution. Beijing's intent was not to cure cancer but to examine the possibility of immunizing their population against radiation poisoning in a nuclear war.[7]

The CCP is playing for keeps, and they are coming after the United States. Our duty as Americans is not only to prevent a hot war but to follow in the footsteps of our fathers, mothers, and grandparents by overcoming tyranny in our generation. I cannot improve upon Ronald Reagan's simple vision: "We win. They lose."[8]

IMPERIALISM STRIKES BACK

I N ONE OF HISTORY'S amusing episodes, the immediate cause
of the Berlin Wall's collapse was the incompetence of a
communist bureaucrat. Throughout 1989, East Germans
were fleeing the Soviet Bloc as travel restrictions gradually
lifted throughout Europe. The German Democratic Republic
(GDR) eventually bowed to the inevitable and sketched out an
orderly process for emigration. Günter Schabowski, the GDR
spokesperson, was tasked with announcing these plans at a 6
p.m. press conference on November 9, 1989. It must have been
uncomfortable for a Soviet apparatchik to brief journalists in a
Western-style presser. Even more ironic, Schabowski's historic
mistake was one Washington politicians make all the time: he
didn't read his briefing materials.[1]

Instead of explaining the actual plan—that East Germans
could apply for passports the following day—the spokesperson of the East German government announced, in effect, the
instant collapse of the Iron Curtain: "We have decided today to
implement a regulation that allows every citizen of the German

Democratic Republic to leave the GDR through any of the border crossings . . . immediately, without delay."[2] Almost as amusing as the gaffe itself was Schabowski's hope that "the movement will regulate itself."[3] It certainly did—in the form of 2 million East Germans crossing that bright line between tyranny and freedom over the next few days.[4]

Back in Washington, another press conference was playing out—this one in the Oval Office with President George H. W. Bush. The president's measured demeanor contrasted with the striking footage of a collapsed wall and exuberant celebrations in West Berlin. When the American press asked Bush why he wasn't more excited, the president quipped, "I'm elated. I'm just not an emotional kind of guy."[5]

Bush was gently guiding the Soviet Union's path to history's ash heap, but he didn't pull any punches four months later when his administration published the 1990 National Security Strategy: "The challenge of an aggressive, repressive Soviet Union was contained by a system of alliances, which we helped create, and led. In this historic endeavor, America has succeeded—brilliantly."[6] *Contained*, the operative word in the president's preamble, was a reference to the broad contours of American grand strategy from 1945 to the Soviet Union's dissolution. Containment was based on the assessment of State Department strategist George Kennan that "Soviet society may well contain deficiencies which will eventually weaken its own total potential." This assumption called for "a policy of firm containment," in hopes that these internal contradictions would eventually hamstring Soviet strength.[7] It was a good bet that resulted in one of America's greatest triumphs. The loose lips of a communist bureaucrat may have lit the spark that consumed the Soviet Union, but America had been pouring kerosene for decades.[8]

That same year, however, the United States faced early warnings from its next adversary, the PRC. In the midst of America's Cold War triumph, Washington committed one of its greatest foreign policy failures. The impacts of this failure wouldn't be fully felt until decades later—in fact, today, as America finds itself hamstrung by a threat largely of its own making.

"YES, BUT . . . ": THE ORIGINS OF AMERICA'S MISGUIDED CHINA POLICY

Five months before the wall fell, university students in Beijing petitioned their own government for freedom and democratic reforms. The demonstrations came to a point in Tiananmen Square, the cultural center of China, with students occupying the area for weeks. The response of the PRC was the mirror opposite of Schabowski's bungled presser. Instead of bending to popular will, the PLA rolled out the tanks and made mincemeat of student demonstrators on June 3–4. The account from the British embassy in Beijing was especially chilling: the PLA "ran over" civilians at 65 kilometers per hour "time and time again to make quote pie unquote," "collected [human bodies] by bulldozer," "incinerated [the remains] then hosed down drains," and "shot up" ambulances trying to save injured students.[9] To this day, the total number of casualties remains unknown. Most sources estimated a few thousand deaths, but some counts surpass 10,000.[10] Those the PLA couldn't kill immediately were subsequently rounded up and arrested with the aid of security cameras designed and manufactured by Pelco and Siemens Plessey—American and British tech companies, respectively.[11]

The following day, Bush held a press conference. Instead of condemning the CCP and standing squarely with the protestors, the American president called for "reasoned, careful action" instead of an "emotional response."[12] Those remarks formally inducted the "yes, but" China policy into America's repertoire. True, the United States "strongly deplored" the CCP's brutality and slapped Beijing with sanctions and other penalties "to demonstrate our displeasure," but that was the bare minimum. "At the same time," the Bush administration explained, "we have sought to avoid a total cutoff of China's ties to the outside world. Those ties not only have strategic importance, both globally and regionally; they are crucial to China's prospects for regaining the path of economic reform and political liberalization. China's angry isolation would harm all of these prospects."[13]

The result of America's "yes, but" China policy was predictable. After a two-year hiatus, the World Bank not only increased its projects throughout China; it funded the installation of the same security cameras that tracked the Tiananmen protestors—only this time in Tibet, where the CCP was cracking down on Buddhism and sinicizing a region that was supposedly guaranteed semi-autonomy. No matter that Lhasa, Tibet's capital, had minimal traffic congestion, which was the ostensible purpose for the cameras.[14] The West was all too happy to turn a blind eye to the party's brutality because, after all, speaking out would only make things worse. President George H. W. Bush said as much in his reflections on Tiananmen Square: "For this understandably proud, ancient, and inward-looking people, foreign criticism (from peoples they still perceived as 'barbarians' and colonists untutored in Chinese ways) was an affront, and measures taken against them a return to the corrections of the past."[15]

Put aside, for a moment, the odd phrasing of equating "Chinese ways" with violent crackdowns, and the overly simplistic caricature of China as "inward-looking." In 1989, that pivotal year of global affairs, America encountered two wildly different events: the fall of the Berlin Wall and the atrocities of Tiananmen Square. The former presaged the waning of the Cold War, while the latter previewed the waxing of America's next great power adversary. Yet Washington responded exactly the same way to both episodes: hold back, don't gloat, keep U.S. options open. Why? True, Washington had made inroads to Beijing since 1972 to outflank the Soviet Union both geographically and ideologically—but with the USSR's impending collapse, why bother treating China with kid gloves? Put more directly: Why did the United States effectively aid in the construction of China's "Great Firewall"—its infamous surveillance and censorship apparatus—after collapsing the Berlin Wall?

THE "END OF HISTORY" AND THE DECAY OF AMERICAN POWER

Victory is a potent cocktail. In the wake of the Soviet Union's dissolution, America quickly drank away its sobriety. Like actual drunks, inebriated nations have a tendency to document their delusions. One such account comes from Francis Fukuyama, who penned the now infamous essay "The End of History?," published in the *National Interest* magazine in 1989. Fukuyama, a brilliant man, misread the moment when he posited the final triumph of Western ideology for all time: "What we may be witnessing is not just the end of the Cold War, or the passing of a particular period of postwar history, but the end of history as such: that is, the end point of mankind's ideological evolution and the universalization of Western liberal democracy as the final form of human government."[16]

How could anyone know such a thing? Fukuyama pointed not only to the demise of the Soviet Union but also to the "infection" of China with liberalism. Fukuyama heralded the market-oriented reforms of Deng Xiaoping and the receding primacy of communist ideology in Chinese politics. Most striking was his characterization of the Tiananmen student protests as "only the beginning of what will inevitably be mounting pressure for change in the political system."[17] The world is still waiting for that change more than three and a half decades later.

Even so, the triumphalist fervor spread, and policymakers began to believe deeply misguided things about the world in which they lived. Consider President Bill Clinton's stunning declaration in 1994 that "our goals of enhancing our security, bolstering our economic prosperity, and promoting democracy are mutually supportive." Why? Because "nations with growing economies and strong trade ties are more likely to feel secure and to work toward freedom."[18] Americans began to believe they were living in a world without tradeoffs, where free trade and free societies inevitably went hand in hand. It was the dictators who faced a zero-sum choice: reform, or perish. This was the "new world order" George H. W. Bush spoke of before Congress in 1990:

> A new era—freer from the threat of terror, stronger in the pursuit of justice and more secure in the quest for peace. An era in which the nations of the world, east and west, north and south, can prosper and live in harmony. A hundred generations have searched for this elusive path to peace, while a thousand wars raged across the span of human endeavor, and today that new world is struggling to be born. A world quite different from the one we've known. A world where the rule of law supplants the rule of the jungle. A world in which nations recognize the

shared responsibility for freedom and justice. A world where the strong respect the rights of the weak.[19]

For many Americans today, the phrase "new world order" reeks of conspiracy theories about globalist cliques plotting the establishment of a one-world government. The actual truth is more disturbing: American elites believed a lie. They thought they could remake the world in Washington's image and sought to do so from Kuwait and Somalia to Bosnia and Serbia. The 1990s was a decade of decadent dreams, when presidents and pundits sought to make war unthinkable and, in so doing, relegate not just the Soviet Union but illiberalism to the ash heap of history.

It was through this quixotic prism that America viewed the tragedy of Tiananmen Square. The defeat of dictators was a foregone conclusion: dollars and cents were more powerful than battleships and tanks in this new world order. The most powerful people in the world were convinced they could catechize tyrants into democrats. It was the high-water mark of liberal internationalism, the belief that international politics could be defined in its essence by peace and cooperation instead of conflict and war. This delusion reached its zenith at the turn of the millennium.

THE STORIES WE TELL OURSELVES

On September 19, 2000, then-senator Joseph R. Biden strode through the Senate cloakroom and entered Capitol Hill's upper chamber. The world's greatest deliberative body was debating America's China policy—specifically, whether to officially decouple China's human rights performance from America's trading terms with Beijing. Biden, the soon-to-be chair of the Senate Committee on Foreign Relations, was one of the bellwether foreign policy voices in Congress. As it turned out, he was hours away from taking a bellwether vote for U.S.-China relations.

In retrospect, it was an unfair fight. On one side, Fortune 500 giants from the auto, oil, and manufacturing industries poured millions into their lobbying campaign for permanent normal trade relations (PNTR) with China. Opposing big industry were human rights advocates and economic protectionists—neither of which had the wind at their back in globalization's heyday.

Although Biden was inclined to support PNTR, he understood the concerns of his political opponents and was poignantly aware of the CCP's abysmal track record on human rights. But the senator from Delaware was also unique: his approach to the PRC did not rest primarily on commerce or values, but on eschatology. "The search for a truly modern China," Biden explained when he reached the Senate floor,

> is now more than a hundred years old . . . It argu-
> ably began at the turn of the last century with the col-
> lapse of the Qing Dynasty and the birth of the Republic
> of China under Sun Yat-sen. The search has continued
> through Japanese invasion, a bloody civil war, the unmit-
> igated disaster of the Great Leap Backwards, the social
> and political upheaval of the Cultural Revolution, and
> now through two decades of economic opening to the
> outside world.
>
> Viewed in this context, a vote for permanent normal
> trade relations says that we welcome the emergence of a
> prosperous, independent China on the world stage. It also

says we want China to be subject to stronger, multilateral rules of economic behavior—rules about international trade that will influence the structure of their internal, social, economic, and political systems.[20]

Politics is, in large part, storytelling. The best stories, the ones we know and love, have three acts: setup, confrontation, and resolution. Notice the narrative Biden weaved:

- Act 1 (Setup): China's dynastic system collapses. A republic rises, with the possibility of democracy and integration.
- Act 2 (Confrontation): Japanese imperialism and Chinese communism threaten China's democratic, integrated future.
- Act 3 (Resolution): Washington welcomes Beijing into the modern world, an action that will bring about the modern China so many have been seeking for so long.

Like all stories, Biden's plotline rested on a few key assumptions:

- Imperialism is a relic of the past.
- Democracy is the political system of modernity.
- Communism is completely at odds with modernism.
- The CCP is serious about "reforming" and "opening up" to the outside world.
- Inviting China into the international community will modernize China and make it look like America.

Five years later, Republicans were singing from the same hymnal. On September 21, 2005, then–deputy secretary of state Robert Zoellick traveled to New York City to give the keynote address at the annual National Committee on U.S.-China Relations gala. Zoellick's speech reprised Biden's question and asked what comes next for China. His thesis was simple: China's political elites had rejected ideological extremism and embraced globalization. In other words, the plan was working. Zoellick proceeded to sketch President George W. Bush's vision to bring Beijing into modernity: "From China's perspective, it would seem that its national interest would be much better served by working with us to shape the future international system.... We now need to encourage China to become a responsible stakeholder in the international system . . . [in which] China would be more than just a member—it would work with us to sustain the international system that has enabled its success."[21] America's China policy rested on that core belief: the end of history meant the end of enemies. Successive U.S. administrations and members of Congress from both parties believed that global trade and international institutions would not only constrain China's revisionist desires but also tame its government over time. In the wake of the Cold War, the aim of America's relations with China—civilizing Beijing—persisted as a rare enclave of bipartisan agreement.

Narratives are comforting, especially when they tell us what we want to hear. But the true test of politics is policy, and we judge stories by the results of believing in them. As Senator Daniel Patrick Moynihan, Biden's New York colleague at the time, once quipped, "Everyone is entitled to his own opinion, but not to his own facts."[22] What, then, has come of the United States believing this narrative for the past two and a half decades? Are China's dynastic days over? Has the CCP reformed politically as China has grown wealthier? Does the country's political system resemble America's in any discernible way?

Who better to answer this question than Xi Jinping?

★★★★★

Thirteen years after Biden's remarks on the Senate floor, Xi gained the reins of power in China. Eight years after that, Biden assumed the presidency in America. But Xi's and Biden's relationship goes back to the Obama administration, when Biden began cultivating personal ties with China's heir apparent. Biden often brags about traveling 17,000 miles and holding 24 hours of private meetings with Xi as vice president. Dubious though the claims may be, they underscore what should have been a dream come true for Biden: someone he knew and could work with to make Biden's vision for China a reality. Xi Jinping, however, had other dreams.[23]

Upon assuming the rank of chairman of the PRC in March 2013, Xi laid out his vision for China's future.[24] The crux of his agenda is the "China Dream," his plan for a party-led national rejuvenation: "To realize the China Dream, we must take our own path, which is the path of building socialism with Chinese characteristics. It is not an easy path. We are able to embark on this path thanks to the great endeavors of reform and opening up made in the past 30 years and more, the continuous quest made in the 60-plus years of the People's Republic of China, a thorough review of the evolution of the Chinese nation in its 170-plus years of modern history, and carrying forward the 5,000-plus years of Chinese civilization."[25] Xi's "China Dream" is riddled with riddles. It is cloaked in historical references his audience was sure to understand but few outsiders could follow. Unlike Biden's version, it has four acts:

- Act 1 (Setup): China's longstanding greatness in the dynastic era ("5,000-plus years of Chinese civilization").
- Act 2 (Rising Action): China's humiliation at the hand of Western powers during the Opium Wars ("170-plus years of modern history").
- Act 3 (Crisis): China's need for a savior. Mao Zedong helped China "stand up" ("60-plus years of the People's Republic of China"), and Deng Xiaoping helped China grow rich ("reform and opening up"), but China was not yet great again.
- Act 4 (Resolution): Xi Jinping leads the CCP in restoring China's greatness.[26]

With these words, Xi declared war on the world America had built, the beliefs that underpin that world, and the stories that perpetuate it. Whereas American politicians treat imperialism as a discarded relic of history, Xi looks back to China's dynasties with aspiration, not aversion. Many Western leaders have attempted to coax China into "modernity," a word Xi only understands in relation to China's victimization at the hands of European powers. To the CCP, modernity is a word wielded as a weapon for Western interests. Resolving this tension, for Xi, means nothing less than restoring China's greatness under the party's leadership. According to Michael Schuman, a contributing writer at the *Atlantic*, Xi's obsession with "greatness" is a dark omen for the world: "China was the dominant power in Asia for very, very, very long stretches of time over the last two thousand years. When . . . Xi Jinping talks about China and what's happening in China today, he describes it as a rejuvenation, or return, or a restoration. He often says in his speeches that China was a great power, and China will be a great power again."[27] In other words, the answer lies in the first act of Xi's story, the very act most Americans and many Westerners ignore. This is a grave error, because Xi's "China Dream" doesn't just spring from contemporary history. It flows from China's larger story, which spans from modernity back to antiquity. The message is unmistakable: imperialism is not dead. Xi views the CCP as akin to past dynasties in its governing power over China. By extension, Xi is the latest in a long line of emperors presiding over a timeless empire, making the party the singular force of China's national and civilizational redemption. As such, it alone can restore China's rightful and exalted status and will do so in a way that transcends modern ideological concepts about democracy or liberalism. Xi's China is a resurgent imperial power.

Since Xi Jinping's ascendency to the post of general secretary in 2012, the CCP has built and militarized artificial islands in the South China Sea,[28] sparred with India along its de facto border, encroached into Bhutan's sovereign territory, and continued to threaten Taiwan with invasion.[29] Internally, Xi has overseen an ongoing genocide against Uyghur Muslims in Xinjiang, the PRC's westernmost region.[30] The CCP has also broken international treaties and eliminated political freedoms in Hong Kong, jailing activists and suppressing free speech. Across the world, the party employs similar tactics to silence dissent and shape favorable discourse. These are not the actions of a "responsible stakeholder." In fairness, the CCP of

Zoellick's day was less brazen in its efforts to undercut America. At the time, the rhetoric of "peaceful rise" and "peaceful development" dominated Beijing's diplomacy—and Washington fell for the ruse.

Indeed, America has been slow to respond. The CCP's ongoing and pervasive theft of American intellectual property initially caught Washington's attention. By some estimates, U.S. companies lose hundreds of billions of dollars each year to PRC-backed economic espionage.[31] Eventually, U.S. lawmakers noticed Confucius Institutes, PRC-funded outposts across American universities that censored classroom discussion about the party's human rights abuses and created financial incentives for colleges across the United States to cooperate with their PRC counterparts on dual-use research. Red lights started flashing when Washington began to realize the human rights implications of doing business in China—namely, censoring search results and providing technology to surveillance companies. In many instances, U.S. companies were the eyes and ears and hands and feet of the CCP within China. Instead of changing China, the CCP was changing America. With the benefit of hindsight, America's mission to civilize the CCP seems flawed and hubristic. Instead of changing the CCP, we supercharged the growth of our greatest strategic adversary since the Soviet Union.

Napoleon is said to have once famously warned, "Let China sleep, for when she wakes, she will shake the world." Under Xi Jinping's rule, the CCP is not only shaking the world; it is dousing the foundations of the American-backed global order with kerosene. That alone is bad enough, but the party is out for more than sabotage. Beijing is building a new world order of its own. The details of Xi's vision are new, but it is rooted in China's centuries-long quest for greatness. If America is to turn the tables and prevail in this new cold war, we must begin by understanding the story Xi and the CCP are telling themselves. It starts and ends with imperialism.

CHAPTER 2

FROM TIME IMMEMORIAL

WHEN RICHARD NIXON defied expectations and went to China in 1972, Henry Kissinger, his national security adviser, packed the president's briefcase. Among Nixon's reading materials was *The Chinese Looking Glass*, a book by British journalist Dennis Bloodworth about understanding China on its own terms.[1] In his opening pages, Bloodworth sets the stage by going back to the beginning: "The gaudy catalogue of China's disasters and dynastic glories, whose monumental scale has given the Chinese much of their character ... brings us to our true beginning."[2] Kissinger, one of America's most consequential foreign policy leaders in recent memory, clearly internalized the centrality of China's "true beginning." In his 2011 tome *On China*, Kissinger marveled at China's "singularity" and staying power.[3] Indeed, even the hardest of hearts cannot help but be moved by the continuity of a civilization that predates the birth of Christ by hundreds, even thousands, of years.

Awe, however, is no substitute for knowledge. In the opening pages of *On China*, Kissinger writes of China's "splendid

isolation" that cultivated "a satisfied empire with limited territorial ambition."[4] The historical record, however, does not vin-
dicate Kissinger. It contradicts him. From the Qin dynasty's
founding in 221 BC to the Qing's collapse in AD 1912, China's
sovereign territory expanded by a factor of four. What began as
a small nation bound in the fertile crescent of the Yangtze and
Yellow Rivers morphed into an imperial wrecking ball. In the
words of Bloodworth, the very author Kissinger recommended
to Nixon in 1972, "It would be absurd to pretend that the Chinese had never been greedy for ground—they started life in the
valley of the Yellow River and ended by possessing a gigantic
empire."[5] It was yet another case of government officials failing
to read their briefing materials.[6]

To be sure, China was not the aggressor in every war it
fought.[7] In antiquity, nomadic tribes regularly raided China's
protodynasties. During the infamous Opium Wars of the
nineteenth century, Western imperialist powers victimized
and preyed upon China at gunpoint. The CCP regularly refers
to China's "Century of Humiliation," when European empires
brutalized China and killed or wounded tens of thousands
of Chinese men, women, and children. Indeed, the party has
memorialized these grievances in a permanent exhibit of the
National Museum of China, just steps away from Tiananmen
Square.[8]

For all of Beijing's legitimate and long-standing security
concerns, however, the sheer scope of China's expansion is
undeniable. Western leaders often deny or ignore it, usually
at the behest and prodding of Chinese leaders. When Nixon
finally gained an audience with Mao Zedong, he reassured the
chairman, "We know China doesn't threaten the territory of
the United States." Mao quickly corrected him: "Neither do we

threaten Japan or South Korea." To which Nixon added, "Nor any country."[9] Within the decade, Beijing invaded Vietnam.

At the time, Nixon's gambit was to split the Soviet bloc and drive a wedge between the Soviet Union and the People's Republic of China. Nixon and Kissinger saw the Sino-Soviet split and took stock of the PRC's trajectory: a growing population that, once harnessed, was poised to dominate the global economy. It was textbook realpolitik: cold, dispassionate tactics divorced from moralism. If Washington could turn the Soviet Union's junior partner, the West could significantly hamper Moscow's ability to project power into Eastern Europe and Southeast Asia.

During the final years of Nixon's life, his presidential speechwriter William Safire asked him about that fateful trip to Beijing in 1972. Had opening up to the PRC made Americans safer and China freer? According to Safire, "That old realist, who had played the China card to exploit the split in the Communist world, replied with some sadness that he was not as hopeful as he had once been: 'We may have created a Frankenstein.'"[10] Eventually, as we will see, many in the United States came to realize this predicament. Unfortunately, articulating that problem well has proven difficult.

HOW USELESS CLICHÉS ORIENTALIZE CHINA

During her brief stint as director of policy planning at the State Department in 2019, Kiron Skinner previewed the shop's keystone intellectual project: a strategy to counter China, in the spirit of George Kennan's "containment" strategy. At a public event in April 2019, Skinner tipped her hand and revealed her philosophy of U.S.-China competition: "This is a fight with a really different civilization and a different ideology, and the United States hasn't had that before." She went on to add, incorrectly, "It's the first time that we will have a great power competitor that is not Caucasian."[11] Skinner received widespread criticism for these remarks and was soon after dismissed for unrelated issues.

Skinner's mistake was twofold. First, she simply got the history wrong and ignored Imperial Japan in World War II. Of deeper consequence was her failure to explain what strategic culture actually is, why it matters, and how China's past shapes the CCP's behavior today. In fairness, these errors aren't unique to Skinner. Understanding Chinese history can be difficult for most Westerners. In some ways, it's difficult to think of two more different nations:

- The United States is less than three hundred years old. China was unified more than two hundred years before Christ was born.
- Immigrants founded America. Denizens established China.
- The United States was born out of revolution against a colonial power. China came into being from a regional conflict of gigantic proportions.
- Favorable geography allowed America to grow economically and territorially on its own terms and at its own pace. China came into being surrounded by rival kingdoms and tribes on every side.

Americans turn to one source more than any other to make sense of these differences: *The Art of War* by Sun Tzu. One of his more recognizable dictums, "All warfare is based on deception," has captured the imagination of many Western thinkers who, by virtue of their Eurocentric history, tend to think of warfare as force-on-force contests.[12] Sun Tzu's assertion that "supreme excellence consists in breaking the enemy's resistance without fighting" also challenges American understanding of a bright line between wartime and peacetime.[13]

Instead of investigating the history that informed Sun Tzu's counsel, however, many policymakers take the easier path of orientalizing China. "China thinks in centuries, and America thinks in decades" is a pervasive platitude. Another well-meaning but vapid cliché is "America plays chess, but China plays Go." Both games define victory differently: the objective of chess is capturing the king, while the goal of Go is strategic encirclement. Even so, those factual statements are often left untethered from history and offered as self-evident axioms. What we're left with are useless clichés that offer no actual understanding of why Chinese strategists advised cunning and deception, or how China's unique historical experiences informed military tactics.[14] In the absence of curiosity, an impression easily forms of China as "the other," a mysterious, inscrutable competitor. A shallow understanding of Beijing's past story leads to incomplete conclusions about its present behavior. More often than not, policymakers find it easier to avoid China's history entirely. In late 2020, the Policy Planning office finished the seventy-two-page report. It was a commendable attempt to reprise Kennan's strategic clarity, but China's dynastic strategic culture received a single page of attention.[15]

Reducing strategic culture to vague racial differences helps no one except Xi Jinping and the Chinese Communist Party. The CCP works to enmesh itself with the Chinese people and regularly uses them as a rhetorical human shield. To criticize the CCP, according to the well-worn rhetorical trope of

Beijing's diplomats, is to "hurt the feelings of 1.4 billion people." As a matter of course, Beijing uses this specious logic to construe anti-CCP policies as evidence of racism. Years before former president Donald Trump fell headlong into this trap with his careless rhetoric about the "Chinese virus" and "kung-flu," a young generation of China hawks had vowed to evade this pitfall. *Washington Post* columnist Josh Rogin wrote about this resolve in his 2020 bestseller *Chaos under Heaven*, which documented the collective decision of Washington, DC–based China hands to blunt Beijing's attempts "to divide Americans by party or ethnicity, to divert attention from its actions."[16] I was a regular member of those meetings and still believe America's leaders must differentiate the party from the Chinese people—not only out of respect for those who daily live under the CCP's jackboot but also for the safety of Chinese Americans, who faced a rise of race-based crime in the wake of the COVID-19 pandemic. But, in doing so, we must avoid a separate trap: equating the party with China.

MANIFEST ENTITLEMENT:
THE MIDDLE KINGDOM'S STRATEGIC CULTURE

China's history did not begin in 1949 when Mao Zedong and the CCP established the PRC. Nor did it start with China's "Century of Humiliation," when European imperialist powers forcibly opened China in the mid-nineteenth century. Chinese civilization predates America and the West by orders of millennia. That context gives meaning to the party's contemporary behavior. The themes of greatness, fall, and restoration hidden in Xi's remarks in 2017 constitute the essence of Chinese history. They are the four-act play of China's story, or "strategic culture"—without which it is impossible to understand the

CCP's strategy today. Strategic culture explains how a country's unique experiences shape distinct national identities that translate into foreign policy. These three elements—story, identity, and policy—reinforce and shape one another.[17] To be sure, the CCP has its own story, identity, and policies, but the party is one tributary in a long river. American leaders cannot prevail against the CCP without understanding the story and identity that belong to China.

A full exposition of China's strategic culture eclipses the scope of this book, but cursory examination reveals millennia of political steadiness that illuminates Beijing's conduct today. From the start, China has been a civilizational juggernaut striving for political hegemony. China has often attempted to conceal this ambition with conciliatory diplomacy, but its neighbors know from experience the struggle to live—and survive—in the dragon's shadow. CCP diplomats often bully China's neighbors by claiming sovereignty over part or all of their territory "from time immemorial"—an inadvertent admission that the party is the latest crusader in a long line of imperialists.[18] This struggle that was once relegated to the nations of East Asia is now a challenge for every country in the world.

Zhongguo: The Middle Kingdom

The first record of China's name dates back to a pottery inscription from the Zhou dynasty, more than three thousand years ago. It reads, "live here in the central area of the world [zhai zi zhongguo]." A more literal interpretation was "to live in the center of the kingdom."[19] Over time, however, zhongguo took on a broader meaning, with geography playing a significant role.

Located in a river basin sandwiched among the Gobi Desert to the north, a series of mountain ranges to the west, and the mighty Yangtze River to the south, China was a thriving agricultural economy in as early as 2000 BC. This topographic cradle gave the early Chinese people something their nomadic neighbors rarely possessed: a stable livelihood and a flourishing society. From written language and agricultural advancements to philosophy and prosperity, China was the definition of civilization in its neighborhood.[20] The fact that northern Turkic Mongols regularly raided Chinese settlements to steal food and possessions was an implicit recognition of China's economic and social superiority. Whether for good or bad, surrounding peoples streamed into China to get a piece of it.[21]

As China's standard of living outpaced those of surrounding regions, Chinese political elites began to acquire a superiority complex. According to Michael Schuman, "The Chinese did not confront any other society with the same degree of political and economic organization or level of literacy. . . . So far as the people of the Zhou could tell, their civilization was superior to any other. They were the super elite, their kingdom a superpower."[22] Over time, *zhongguo* became a statement of cultural primacy and an explicit claim to civilizational hegemony. Insiders were civilized, and outsiders were barbarians. By the time of the Qing dynasty, China's name denoted global centrality. *Zhongguo* no longer meant the center of China, but the center of the world: quite literally, the "Middle Kingdom." For thousands of years, the Chinese have seen their land and empire as center stage in global affairs. Eventually, China's cultural strength would translate into stark political claims.

Tianxia: "All Under Heaven"

China's initial conflict was with steppe nomads, but the geographic scope of authority that early Chinese feudal lords claimed was not restricted to the Yellow River valley. It stretched out in all directions. Over time, the idea of the Middle Kingdom's authority over "all under heaven," or *tianxia*, solidified. Again, geopolitics brings clarity. In its infancy, China lacked natural borders to guard its vaunted civilization. There was broad recognition that security demanded buffer zones in all directions. Bulwarks took multiple forms, either natural or man-made. Some were defensive, like the Great Wall; many others, as we will see, were offensive. Power, not security, was the overriding logic behind *tianxia*.

But *tianxia* was more than a power play. It was an ideological claim, almost religious in nature. If *zhongguo* was a statement of civilizational superiority, then *tianxia* was China's mission of spreading its cultural values beyond its borders. International relations scholar Asım Doğan was not far off when he characterized it as "a salvationist approach" to foreign policy.[23] Two-time Pulitzer Prize nominee Howard W. French came to the same conclusion in 2018: "A sense of manifest Chinese entitlement . . . is implicit in the very phrase *tianxia*."[24]

Importantly, the scope of *tianxia* was without theoretical limit. In the words of Chinese political scientist Yan Xuetong, "Given the then lack of a modern science of understanding geography, the Chinese notion of *all under heaven* meant all the land, sea, and people under heaven. The term *all under heaven* was virtually synonymous with *the world*."[25] Of course, China is not unique in its quest for world domination. Various European states jostled for colonies as they sought to build empires upon which the sun never set—essentially, *tianxia* by a different name. But the signing of the Treaty of Westphalia in 1648 marked the West's slow but steady departure from empire-building. For the vast majority of Western nations today, sovereignty and the nation-state go hand in hand. The German government governs the German people, and so on for the French, British, and everyone else. But if Yan is right, that *all under heaven* encompasses the entire globe, then there is no internal limiting principle to the political influence that China seeks. As we will see throughout this chapter, China never yielded that belief and has never stopped struggling to realize it.

"The Mandate of Heaven": Chinese Political Legitimacy

China's conception of its rulers matched its lofty political aspirations. Millennia before China was united into its first dynasty, feudal princes began calling themselves the "son of heaven." There was, however, the rather obvious problem of multiple warlords claiming to be heaven's one and only son. From roughly 771 BC to 221 BC (the "Spring and Autumn" and "Warring States" eras of China's history), Chinese politics devolved into a Darwinian fight for survival and supremacy. The warfare and intrigue during these periods were staggering, and the death toll rose well into the millions.

Finally, in 221 BC, the state of Qin succeeded in conquering its rivals and, for the first time, unified all of China under one emperor. By unifying the heartland, the Qin ruler proved his worthiness to rule China and gained the "Mandate of Heaven." This concept, which Stanford University professor Charles Hucker calls "the cornerstone of all Chinese political theory," also comprises China's understanding of foreign policy: closing the gap between civilizational greatness (*zhongguo*) and political power (*tianxia*).[26] When that gap was small, China was strong abroad in both influence and territory, and secure at home with legitimacy and peace. When emperors failed to bridge that chasm, however, the Middle Kingdom's foundations grew unstable. China's quest to rule or at least influence all under heaven often risked overstretch and placed massive burdens on the people.

In this way, the Mandate of Heaven was a bottom-up reality in Chinese politics, not merely a top-down imposition of order. The mandate was not granted via free and fair elections, nor bestowed via a "divine right of kings," but seized by way of revolution and effective governance. Legitimacy was largely a product of performance. For the "son of heaven," this meant that his tenure as emperor was always an open question. As Dennis Bloodworth put it, "the principle of the Mandate of Heaven provides that revolution is hallowed by its own success. There is, therefore, always recourse to revolt."[27]

Confucianism: Diplomacy in Chinese Foreign Policy

Whereas Americans are accustomed to an egalitarian society defined by equality, the Chinese built a culture defined by hierarchy. Submission to authority and embracing one's lot in life served as a sort of societal glue. According to Confucianism, the most influential philosophy in China's history, society consists of five relationships: the ones between emperor and subjects, father and son, older brother to younger brother, husband to wife, and friend to friend. In this hierarchical structure, the male-dominated family was the core institution in Chinese society, but all authority filtered upward to the emperor, the enlightened son of heaven. And just as the emperor sat atop China's social pecking order, it was only right for China to sit atop the nations of the world.

Confucianism fed China's superiority, and the Middle Kingdom came to see its neighbors as cultural barbarians to be civilized and enlightened. According to China scholar June Teufel Dreyer, "Confucian society did not conceive of a China, or of a Chinese civilization: there was only civilization and barbarism, with one defining another. What was not civilized was barbaric."[28]

When it came to foreign policy, the understanding among China's neighbors was clear: they had responsibilities to the *zhongguo*, chief among which were civilizational deference and political submission. China's method of subordinating its neighbors into a Chinese-led order was the tribute system, wherein foreign sovereigns would prostrate themselves before the son of heaven in exchange for political recognition and lavish financial gifts. As we will see, these financial obligations often strained China's coffers, but in times of peace the tribute system was worth the cost. It reinforced the rightful Confucian order: all under heaven bowing to the Middle Kingdom. As Professor David Kang of the University of Southern California has rightly observed, this hierarchy "was marked as much by cultural achievement as it was by purely military or economic prowess."[29]

Reverence for and imitation of China's culture was the universal standard of international relations. True, Chinese dynasties of old were not sufficiently powerful to rule the whole world. "The emperor," according to Dennis Bloodworth, "was not so much the conqueror of most of the states that bowed to China, as their suzerain, and he often exacted from their rulers little more than homage and tribute."[30] Even so, the tribute system offered the veneer of *tianxia*. As long as foreign nations bowed the knee to the *zhongguo's* political greatness and cultural superiority, it was enough.[31]

Legalism: Coercion in Chinese Foreign Policy

But what of those who refused enlightened leadership? What if the world needs more than education and morals to truly function? These questions constituted the core of China's political philosophy during its Warring States period, when competing states vied for survival and dominance. Confucianism lacked a satisfying answer to warlords who were engaged in calculations of hard power and had no interest in voluntarily submitting to each other.

China's political tradition of legalism took shape during this era and came to fruition when the Qin state conquered its competitors in 221 BC. In this moment of unity, China translated its civilizational superiority into political domination by unifying competing kingdoms under one dynasty. After Qin Shi Huang, China's first emperor, established his empire, he set about translating political unity into practical unity by standardizing language, roads, and state administration. But he didn't stop there.

The same year he unified China, Emperor Qin Shi Huang attacked southern tribes in the modern-day Chinese provinces of Zhejiang, Guangdong, and Fujian.[32] In 215 BC, in response to tribal threats from his northern border, the emperor sent 300,000 soldiers into modern-day Inner Mongolia, where he annexed additional territory and ordered the construction of the Great Wall.[33] Shortly thereafter, he attacked northern Vietnam.[34] In many ways, legalism was a recognition that the world didn't always conform to China's expectations. Sometimes bringing *zhongguo* and *tianxia* into alignment required force.

Even so, the Qin dynasty's tenure was remarkably short, a mere twenty years. Peasants overthrew the emperor for

one simple reason: he ruled like a tyrant. While he standard-
ized transportation and integrated China's economy, the Qin
emperor also instigated a brutal campaign to crush ideological dissent. That dissent was overwhelmingly Confucian in
nature. In his warpath to unify China, Qin Shi Huang repudi-
ated what he saw as Confucianism's failure to accomplish what
only strict governance could achieve. Thus, when he conquered
the final warring state, Qin Shi Huang banned Confucian criticism of his regime and went so far as to burn books and bury
scholars.[35]

In the process, the Qin era revealed legalism's fatal flaw:
it could unify a state, but its barbaric governance destabilized
China. Meanwhile, Confucianism had the opposite problem. It
ordered society well but was silent on statecraft. This tension
has rested at the heart of China's strategic culture for thousands
of years. Terms like "harmony" and "chaos" are loaded words in
China's political lexicon, for they signify the Middle Kingdom's
oscillation between union and disunion, strength and weakness, ascendancy and collapse. China has long needed both
authoritarian power and civic idealism to hold itself together, a
delicate balance of fire and water. Tragically, the quest for heav-
en's "mandate" often propelled dynasties into adopting aggressive foreign policies abroad to prove their legitimacy at home.[36]

VELVET GLOVE, IRON FIST: IMPERIAL CONFUCIANISM

In the early days of the Han dynasty, political elites found
a cunning way to resolve this tension between authoritarian power and civic idealism: they embraced both simultaneously. Returning, yet again, to Bloodworth's *The Chinese
Looking Glass*: "The early emperors 'kicked upstairs' the more
widely known Confucians, but surrounded themselves with

Legalist confidants. Oppressive decrees were drawn up in fine Confucian language, especially where some really dastardly imposition on the long-suffering public had to be clothed in virtuous double talk."[37] Over time, China's emperors fashioned Confucianism into a velvet glove cloaking the iron fist of legalism. Pamela Kyle Crossley, a professor at Dartmouth College, calls this arrangement "Imperial Confucianism" and notes that nearly all of China's dynasties embraced this ideology. "Though authoritarian," Crossley explains, "the empires could claim the intention on the part of rulers and civil servants to guard the welfare of the common people and to seek their moral improvement."[38] When it came to foreign policy, emperors based their political quest for hegemony (*tianxia*) on their deeper claim of civilizational superiority (*zhongguo*). The result was a consistently aggressive and belligerent Middle Kingdom pushing its way into the rest of the world by brute force. As international relations scholar Asım Doğan put it, China's "theoretical Confucian peacefulness, in practice, turned into a bitter 'civilization-barbarian division,' triggered by an arrogant cultural pride."[39]

To be sure, emperors attempted to order their world with the tribute system when they could. After all, the arrangement rebounded to China's benefit not just abroad, but especially at home as evidence of the Mandate of Heaven. According to Doğan, "The Tributary relations and obedience of the neighboring kings further consolidated the legitimacy of the Chinese emperor and gave him considerable prestige as well. The Son of Heaven, responsible for the whole Tianxia, could prove this claim practically from the obedience of foreign authorities.... For consolidating legitimacy and boosting prestige, the tributaries submitted from Confucian states had an important function."[40] But China's "sons of heaven" never hesitated to unleash war when they encountered opposition. This tendency led to China growing inexorably larger over time, the basic reality Kissinger conveniently ignores. What started in the Yellow River valley grew to eventually encompass Manchuria to the northeast, Mongolia to the north, Xinjiang to the northwest, Tibet to the west, and the southern territories. China gained territory through war, lost it in battle, and won it back again with blood.

The tenor of China's dynastic foreign policy was aggressive, even colonial. Just as the Qin dynasty waged wars of expansion in the north and south, the successive Han dynasty continued these campaigns and added new ones. In 109 BC, the Han invaded, annexed, and colonized Dian (modern-day Yunnan province).[41] The next year, they attacked Korea and established a puppet government.[42] The Han also opened up a new front against the Xiongnu tribes to the west (in modern-day Xinjiang) and set up colonial protectorates in central Asia.[43]

The quest for hegemony pervaded successive dynasties. The Sui invaded Korea four times.[44] The Tang solidified Chinese colonies in Xinjiang, expanded its presence to the border of the Persian Empire, and attacked Tibet.[45] The Yuan, a Mongol dynasty, invaded Japan (twice), southern Vietnam, and Burma, and made Thailand a vassal state.[46] The Ming punished numerous rulers of island kingdoms in the South China Sea and Bay of Bengal who bucked the tribute system.[47] The Qing, a Manchu dynasty, committed genocide in central Asia and formally annexed Xinjiang.[48]

To be sure, this is only a part of China's story. Other dynasties, like the Song, failed to reconstitute the territorial glory of their predecessors and presided over a smaller, shrinking

China. But these were exceptions to the larger rule. While dynasties rose and fell, China continued to expand its borders and colonize its neighbors in pursuit of heaven's mandate.[49] In November 2023, American tech billionaire Elon Musk claimed that "the history of China suggests that China is not acquisitive, meaning they are not going to go out and invade a whole bunch of countries."[50] China's actual history reveals a different story. According to the Chinese Academy of Military Sciences, the in-house think tank of the PLA, from 1100 BC to AD 1912 China waged 3,790 wars.[51] On average, dynastic China never knew a year without war.

THE CONTINUITY OF CHINA'S STRATEGIC CULTURE

For all the focus of American strategists on China today, many in Washington miss the true essence of the Middle Kingdom's strategic culture: its continuity. We cannot fully appreciate the party's appetite for world domination merely within the confines of its own existence, for the CCP is behaving like the dynasties that preceded it. Indeed, it has done so for quite some time.

In 1958, Mao cast himself in chilling terms as an even more barbaric and ruthless emperor than Qin strongman Shi Huang: "He only buried 460 scholars alive, while we've buried 46,000. . . . You accuse us of acting like the First Emperor, but you're wrong; we've outdone him 100 times over!"[52] On a separate occasion, Mao credited Qin-era military strategy as influential in his thinking.[53] Several scholars have also noted Mao's outreach to Africa and the Global South and its resonance with *zhongguo* and *tianxia*.[54]

Decades later, when Deng Xiaoping and his comrades were forced to pick up the pieces of Mao's chaotic rule, Deng led

China's historic "reform and opening up" policy, in which China would open its doors to the outside world. Crucially, he made the case for joining the global economy on the basis of China's dynastic past, with specific references to China's final two dynasties, the Ming and the Qing. Deng's historical appeal was evident to his contemporaries: the dynastic system collapsed in large part because of economic isolationism. For the PRC to grow and thrive, integration was nonnegotiable.[55]

In 1997, Jiang Zemin, former leader of China, visited Harvard University and spoke to American students—evidence in itself that Deng's mission to open China had succeeded. In those remarks, Jiang walked America's ivy school elites through the technological advances of the Qin, Han, Tang, Ming, and Qing dynasties. Then, he drew a straight line from the dynastic era to modern China. "China became a vast unified country more than 2,000 years ago," Jiang explained, beckoning young American minds into the vastness of China's existence:

> The deep-rooted Chinese culture become a strong bond for ethnic harmony and national unity. Solidarity and unity have been inscribed in the hearts of the Chinese people as part of their national identity. Despite occasional division in the Chinese history, ethnic harmony and national unity have remained the main stream in the history of the Chinese nation, and an important guarantee for China's development and progress. The founding of the People's Republic of China marked an unprecedented great unity of the Chinese nation.[56]

Nine years later, then-president George W. Bush asked Hu Jintao, Jiang's successor, what kept him awake at night. Hu's response? Creating 25 million jobs a year to keep China's econ-omy growing.[57] His answer revealed more than the difficulty of managing China's path to prosperity; it exposed Hu's anxiety about maintaining the "great unity" of which Jiang spoke. Hu Jintao was terrified of losing the Mandate of Heaven.[58]

As we have already seen, Xi Jinping never misses a chance to bolster his claim to heaven's mandate by appealing to Chi-nese history. Xi turned heads in 2014 when he quoted legalist philosophers of the Qin era to justify his anti-corruption cam-paign: "When those who uphold the law are strong, the state is strong. When they are weak, the state is weak."[59] But Xi is equally quick to boost Confucianism as evidence of China's civilizational superiority. While the West was mired in a "crisis of confidence," the CCP was "the loyal inheritor and promoter of China's outstanding traditional culture."[60]

THERE CAN ONLY BE ONE

What does China's continuity mean for us today? Beijing is approaching the world not to embrace it, but to rule it. The Western world has no excuse for missing this reality, and American politicians have badly misjudged Beijing for decades. The bill for our willful ignorance has now come due, and we have no choice but to face the threat that is the CCP.

As we face reality, we make a grave error by isolating the party from China's history. If Washington is to truly under-stand the sources of China's conduct in the world, policy-makers must remember Sun Tzu's guidance: "If you know the enemy and know yourself, you need not fear the result of a hun-dred battles. If you know yourself but not the enemy, for every victory gained you will also suffer a defeat."[61] America's China policy will continue to be a "two steps forward, one step back" affair until it reckons with the Middle Kingdom's penchant for imperialism. The first act in Xi's story, the one most overlooked by America's political leaders, is by far the least understood and the most important.

This reality calls into question the unspoken objective of American policymakers: seeking a democratic China. For all their differences, both hawks and doves in the United States have framed the "China problem" as an ideological challenge. Proponents of engagement believed that economic contacts would necessarily lead to political reform, a belief rooted in liberal internationalism. Advocates of confrontation couch the CCP regime as the problem, which implies an ideological solution. One unchanging constant in America's China policy since Nixon's meeting with Mao in 1972 is the steady commitment to regime change, either by commerce or competition. The underlying belief in the universal power of democracy has proved intoxicating. "If we can just make them like us," the thinking goes, "we can turn an enemy into a friend."

Perhaps this self-delusion is inevitable. America's national identity is steeped in beliefs about liberty, equality, and opportunity. But the CCP's heritage raises an uncomfortable question for the United States: even if modern China were to become a democracy, would it cease to be the Middle Kingdom? If the CCP collapsed and China followed Taiwan's path of economic and political liberalization, would it suddenly lose its *tianxia*-sized appetite? Maybe. Then again, perhaps simplifying Beijing's behavior to its current Communist Party overlords ignores thousands of years of China's own history, as well as the strategic culture that informs those decisions.[62]

This is no Westphalian state. This is an ancient empire that has always played by its own rules. And, as we will see, the BRI is China's game, played by China's rules. Xi Jinping's goal is strikingly similar to the ambitions of his dynastic predecessors: securing the recognition from all under heaven that China is superior. By definition, a superior China means making the United States inferior. There can only be One Belt and One Road, for there can only be one son of heaven and one Middle Kingdom.

MIDDLE KINGDOM RESURGENT

I N SEPTEMBER 2013, Xi Jinping launched his gambit to change the world. Standing in the conference hall of Nazarbayev University in Kazakhstan's capital city, Astana, Xi spoke of Eurasia's dormant economic potential and revealed his plan to unleash it. "To forge closer economic ties, deepen cooperation and expand development space in the Eurasian region," he declared, "we should take an innovative approach and jointly build an economic belt along the Silk Road."[1] This Silk Road Economic Belt would stretch from China to Europe, with various routes passing through Russia, central Asia, southwest Asia, and the Middle East. Two months later, Xi visited Jakarta and announced the Twenty-First-Century Maritime Silk Road, the Belt and Road Initiative's seafaring component.

Since 2013, the BRI has grown from a Eurasian venture into a global undertaking (see map 1). What started as a land and sea project has expanded to include the Digital Silk Road, the Polar Silk Road, the Health Silk Road, and several other iterations. The projects have likewise spanned from infrastructure and port construction to telecommunications technology and personal protective equipment—the vast majority of which are underwritten by Chinese-backed loans. The BRI has spawned film festivals, diplomatic summits, and business conferences covering all aspects of Xi's five-point outline: policy coordination, transit infrastructure, unimpeded trade, use of local currencies, and people-to-people exchanges.[2]

Geographically, Southeast Asia and central Asia have remained the project's center of gravity, with Africa trailing close behind. Beyond Europe and the Middle East, the BRI has even extended into the Southern Hemisphere, particularly in Latin America and South America. By all accounts, it is the most ambitious global development project in modern history. In the words of Jonathan Hillman, a China expert at the Center for Strategic and International Studies, "the Belt and Road is so big it is almost impossible for one person to have mastery of it. Sometimes I wonder if China grasps the whole thing."[3] The details of the BRI are fuzzy, to be sure, and beyond the scope of this book—but Xi knows exactly what he is doing.[4]

By referencing the Silk Road of antiquity, Xi called back to an era when Eurasia was integrated economically. In his retelling of the landmass's history, "More than 2,000 years of exchanges demonstrate that on the basis of unity, mutual trust, equality, inclusiveness, mutual learning and mutually beneficial cooperation, countries of different races, beliefs and cultural backgrounds are fully capable of sharing peace and development." A benign word salad worthy of a UN speechwriter. But a subsequent editorial on Xinhua, China's state media outlet, captured Xi's message: "Unlike the great sea routes to the New World discovered by the European navigators that prompted

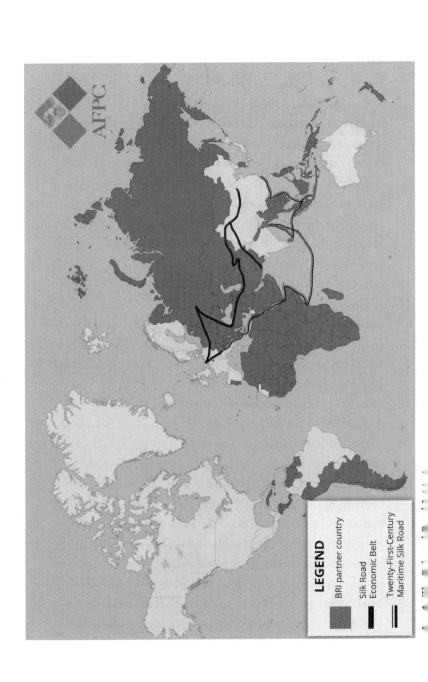

LEGEND

BRI partner country

Silk Road Economic Belt

Twenty-First-Century Maritime Silk Road

AFPC

bloody conquest and colonization, the Silk Road was always a road of peace."[5]

But Beijing's neighbors in Astana and Jakarta knew better.

Xi began his remarks in Kazakhstan by rewinding 2,100 years into the past. He fixated on one character: Zhang Qian, the Han dynasty envoy, who went on multiple "missions of peace and friendship" to central Asia. "Today, as I stand here and look back at that episode of history," Xi mused, "I could almost hear the camel bells echoing in the mountains and see the wisp of smoke rising from the desert."[6] Even so, Xi neglected to recount the purpose of Zhang's forays.

At the command of Emperor Wu Ti of the Han dynasty, who ruled from 141 BC to 87 BC, Zhang traveled nearly four thousand miles to search for military allies against Turkic tribes. At the time, the central Asian kingdoms weren't interested in ganging up with China against their nomadic neighbors. So, after the Han dynasty subdued the tribes and established a protectorate in modern-day Xinjiang, Wu Ti's army continued west and smashed the regimes of modern-day Uzbekistan.[7] The ultimate result of Zhang's diplomacy was China's colonial projects in central Asia.

In Indonesia, Xi told the story of Zheng He, the famed Chinese admiral who sailed seven voyages and "left nice stories of friendly exchanges between the Chinese and Indonesian peoples."[8] What Xi didn't mention was the Ming dynasty's geopolitical purpose for Zheng He's voyages: garnering recognition from the states in China's near-abroad that the *zhongguo* did indeed rule over *tianxia*. Of relevance to Indonesia, the Middle Kingdom's favorite admiral chased, beat, kidnapped, and executed the Sumatran ruler in AD 1415—not just out of personal spite but to reaffirm Chinese suzerainty over the

Malacca Strait.[9] Zheng took tribute and gathered attestations to China's greatness quite literally at gunpoint. Several years after Xi's speech, then–secretary of defense Jim Mattis recognized this implicit threat: "The Ming Dynasty appears to be [China's] model, albeit in a more muscular manner, demanding other nations become tribute states, kowtowing to Beijing; espousing One Belt, One Road . . . and attempting to replicate on the international stage their authoritarian domestic model, militarizing South China Sea features while using predatory economics of piling massive debt on others."[10] This history was not lost on either of Xi's audiences in Kazakhstan or Indonesia. The Western world, however, is largely asleep to the BRI's true nature.

A "*TIANXIA* FEELING": THE CONTEXT OF THE BRI

What kind of world does China want to build? What lies at the end of the Belt and Road? If you ask the pundit class, the answers—much like the BRI itself—are all over the map. For Kent E. Calder, author of *Super Continent: The Logic of Eurasian Integration*, the BRI is nothing more than a "low conflict" system of transcontinental commerce that "is far from a universal 'tributary system.'"[11] Why? Because of the BRI's "'win-win' character for those directly involved."[12] Authors Daniel Drache, A. T. Kingsmith, and Duan Qi take a more even-handed approach in *One Road, Many Dreams: China's Bold Plan to Remake the Global Economy*. "In the final analysis," they claim, "China's global infrastructure initiative is like a giant puzzle with 10,000 pieces that Beijing is patiently assembling, piece by piece, while the West is caught flat-footed."[13] They define that "giant puzzle" as Beijing's quest for energy security, new export markets, and increased geopolitical influence in

Eurasia at Washington's expense.[14] While the BRI's ultimate fate is unknown, these analysts draw a distinction between the United States—an "imperial hegemon" that has repeatedly "interfered" with the sovereignty of many nations—and the PRC, which is "proceed[ing] always cautiously with intense determination."[15] As it turns out, though, the CCP has already answered the question of what kind of world China wants to build, if we would only listen to it.

The heart of Xi Jinping's foreign policy is the "Community of Common Destiny for All Mankind." To Drache, Kingsmith, and Duan, the community is nothing more than the CCP's phrase for globalization: "It is a view of the world that is deeply embedded in China's modern psyche—what occurs on one continent inevitably impacts another."[16] The CCP's own documents about Xi Jinping Thought tell a different story. According to analysis published by Beijing's National Defense University in 2018, "Constructing a Community of Common Destiny for All Mankind . . . is a manifestation of China, as a world power, playing its role as protector of all humankind's shared values."[17] The rhetoric drips with Marxist language and suggests Xi's ambition to create a new world order, one governed and led by the Marxist-Leninist CCP—with Xi at the helm.[18]

Beneath the CCP's ideological dogmatism, the community flows in the ancient current of Chinese imperialism. China scholar Nadège Rolland identified this connection in 2017 when she noted the community "has a taste of 'deja vu.'"[19] She went on to quote a major general in the PLA who spoke of the BRI's "*tianxia* feeling" at Beijing's National Defense University in 2015.[20] She also warned that a "Sinocentric order would require the regional countries' implicit or explicit consent to China's primacy."[21]

Given these realities, the real danger of Xi's vision comes into focus: the community that the CCP is struggling to build is designed to supplant Western values of freedom, democracy, and sovereignty as ordering principles of international relations. In the words of Dan Tobin of the Center for Strategic and International Studies, "The challenge Beijing represents is not to Washington's status in Asia, but to the nature of the global order's predominant values, and the vehicle for that challenge is an effort to build both the physical and intellectual infrastructure underpinning the next phases of globalization."[22] Chinese authorities sought to deflect these concerns when they rebranded the project from the One Belt, One Road (OBOR) initiative to the Belt and Road Initiative (BRI), much like the Hu Jintao–era reversion from China's "peaceful rise" to "peaceful development." As Angela Stanzel of the European Council on Foreign Relations put it, the BRI rebrand "make[s] it sound more like an inclusive initiative rather than a strategy."[23]

Nonetheless, it is a strategy. The Belt and Road may be gilded with rhetoric of "win-win diplomacy," but underneath that veneer is the iron steel of China's resolve to become great again. In one crucial respect, the BRI is even more dangerous than many China scholars initially thought. It is not a neighborhood project, but a global aspiration. For a resurgent empire seeking to reconstitute *tianxia*, it should come as no surprise that the sun never sets over the BRI.

BEIJING'S TWISTED MONROE DOCTRINE: THE BRI IN EAST AND SOUTHEAST ASIA

In 2010, Yang Jiechi, the then–minister of foreign affairs, got into a shouting match with the Singaporean foreign minister and exclaimed, "China is a big country, and other countries are small countries, and that's just a fact."[24] At issue was China's sovereignty claims over the South China Sea, and the unwillingness of the member states of the Association of Southeast Asian Nations (ASEAN) to kowtow to the Middle Kingdom's designs. Three years later, however, Beijing rolled out its dual-track plan to make the South China Sea its own. Through a deft combination of foreign assistance and territorial expansion that would have made the dynasties of old proud, Xi Jinping neutralized strategic opposition from ASEAN without firing a shot.

After Xi's 2013 remarks heralding the BRI in Jakarta, Beijing began funding what has ultimately amounted to $220 billion in infrastructure and investments throughout its neighborhood.[25] The vast majority of these projects are scattered throughout Southeast Asian nations, most of which welcomed the BRI enthusiastically. Laos, one of ASEAN's poorest member states, received more than $22 billion in infrastructure projects and investments from 2013 to 2022.[26] Of particular importance to Laos capital Vientiane was the China-Laos Railway, a flagship project that integrates landlocked Laos into a trade corridor running from Kunming in China's Yunnan province to Thailand's Laem Chabang port.[27] China also provided financing and labor for several highways throughout Laos that significantly cut travel time. Cambodia also richly benefited from China's largesse, to the tune of a new airport in Siem Reap and hydropower plants.[28]

In a conversation with media outlet Xinhua, a Cambodian official praised the BRI as "sincere with no strings attached."[29] If only that were the case. Since 2013, Beijing's strategy in Southeast Asia has been to buy low and sell high. Its investments

in Cambodia and Laos pale in comparison to the BRI's foot-
print in ASEAN's wealthier nations, but it was enough for Xi
Jinping to cash in for the prize he wanted most: neutralizing
ASEAN's opposition to Beijing's territorial advances in its
own backyard.

When Xi launched the BRI, he also let China's state-
owned enterprises loose in the South China Sea. What the
CCP built from 2013 to 2015 shocked the world. Beijing constructed a makeshift archipelago of artificial atolls throughout
the South China Sea, claimed the waters surrounding them as
sovereign PRC territory, and subsequently armed those islands
with missiles, bombers, and radar.[30] China also leveraged its
fishing fleet and eventually its navy to contest the routine economic activities and military patrols of Vietnam, the Philippines, and Malaysia.[31]

In 2016, Xi's plan came full circle. When ASEAN diplomats gathered for their annual summit, Laos held the chair.
Diplomats from nations impacted by Beijing's adventurism
sought to include language condemning China's behavior in
the summit's joint resolution; Cambodia dutifully objected.[32]
Because of ASEAN's requirement for consensus, there was
no statement from the nations most endangered by the CCP's
aggression. By the time ASEAN member states broke the
logjam, it was too late. Beijing's "little blue men" in the South
China Sea were already facts on the ground.

Neither Laos nor Cambodia has territorial waters in the
South China Sea. That was the point. Xi used weaker states
to divide ASEAN from within—while still handsomely benefiting Indonesia, Malaysia, and Singapore with BRI projects of their own. In so doing, Beijing succeeded in locking
in de facto control of the South China Sea at the expense

of the wealthiest Southeast Asian nations while tempering their opposition with economic sweeteners. The CCP also leveraged the poorest nations in ASEAN with infrastructure projects of their own to divide the block, blunting any effective diplomatic response. Unlike America's Monroe Doctrine, which sought to prevent the expansion of external colonialist powers, China is using the BRI in Southeast Asia to grease the skids for its own imperial expansion beyond its near-abroad.

NORMALIZING GENOCIDE: THE BRI IN EURASIA

In the wake of World War I, British geographer and strategist Sir Halford John Mackinder warned his contemporaries that the future of global affairs hinged on the terms of political peace in Eurasia's "heartland." By heartland, Mackinder meant eastern Europe, which was insulated from maritime threats. As the geographer put it in 1919, "Who rules the Heartland commands the World-Island: Who rules the World-Island commands the World."[33]

Historically, Mackinder had a point. It is no accident that this "pivot region" was the epicenter of the German-Russian front in World War II and the dividing line between West and East Germany in the Cold War. From the Baltics and central Europe to the Balkans and Turkey, West and East collide in Eurasia, and the peace has often been tenuous and contested. Nothing illustrates this tension more clearly today than Vladimir Putin's war of aggression in Ukraine.

None of this is lost on Xi Jinping or his strategic planners. Codifying China's greatness in the twenty-first century cannot be done apart from subverting America's historically dominant position across the Eurasian landmass. Ever since 1945,

Washington's overriding strategic objective has been preventing the emergence of a regional power in Europe, the Middle East, and East Asia. The leading candidates for regional hegemony in those respective regions are Russia, Iran, and China. It is no coincidence that the CCP has embraced the Kremlin as a "partnership without limits,"[34] while promising hundreds of billions in financing to the mullahs in Tehran.[35]

But Beijing's designs for Eurasia go beyond bolstering its like-minded neighbors to complicate Washington's grand strategy. Xi's quest for restoring China's global greatness means supplanting the United States as the dominant force across the entirety of Eurasia—in effect, joining East and West together on Beijing's terms. Unlike Putin, however, Xi has a plan to accomplish his interests in "the Heartland" without going to war.

Just as it used the BRI to subvert ASEAN from within, the CCP is running a similar play in Eurasia—but at far higher stakes. Instead of buying off low-income countries, Beijing is seeking to redirect the economic orientation of the world's third largest economy: the European Union. This ambition is not readily apparent in BRI data. European infrastructure and investment deals since 2013 total $84 billion—smaller than China's BRI projects in central Asia, Africa, and the Middle East. Often overlooked, however, is the "shadow BRI," Beijing's investments and deals that aren't branded as part of the "project of the century." Accounting for these transactions reveals a staggeringly different picture in China's overseas lending from 2013 to 2022: $81 billion to the United Kingdom, $46 billion to Germany, and $24 billion to France. China's investments in the UK far exceed the top BRI recipient (Pakistan), and its deals with Germany eclipse Indonesia's second-place status in the BRI.[36] When it comes to the "World-Island," flipping Europe is the CCP's primary objective.

But doing that requires winning everything in between Beijing and Brussels. The CCP envisions three separate trade corridors to unify Eurasia: the China-Mongolia-Russia Corridor, the New Eurasian Land Bridge, and the China–Central Asia–West Asia Economic Corridor. These corridors provide commercial redundancy and, more importantly, maximize participation in the BRI. Their impact on transcontinental trade has been immediate. In 2016, 700 freight trains made the trek from western China to Europe. They operated on four lines and only ran once a week. By 2018, 1,400 such trains crisscrossed Eurasia, running on 19 international lines. According to Xinhua, "The transportation time of China-Europe freight trains departing from the center has been cut from 22 days to 15 days, and that of the routes between China and Central Asia from 66 hours to 44 hours."[37]

The potential economic growth for Eurasian governments is undeniable and could boost trade volumes throughout Asia by $329 billion (a 7.3 percent increase), while increasing trade for the European Union by $133 billion (a 2.6 percent increase).[38] In 2019, the World Bank published a more detailed projection of the BRI's economic impact. Assuming infrastructure projects materialize and border delays are minimized, the World Bank expected states like Pakistan to see a 12.75 percent GDP bump, and economists forecasted increased economic growth in central Asian states like Kyrgyzstan and Tajikistan by 20 percent to more than 30 percent.[39] Recently, China has doubled down on economic ties with these nations, even as trade with Western nations has declined. In 2023, China's exports to BRI countries surpassed its exports to the United States, the European Union, and Japan for the first time.[40]

Beijing has leveraged the promise of economic growth in BRI countries to secure political support for its oppressive policies at home, particularly its genocide of Uyghurs and other ethno-religious minorities in Xinjiang. In response to a United Nations resolution in July 2019, wherein twenty-two countries condemned human rights abuses in Xinjiang, a coalition of fifty ambassadors and representatives responded with a separate resolution praising China's "counter-terrorism" campaign there: "Faced with the grave challenge of terrorism and extremism, China has undertaken a series of counterterrorism and deradicalization measures in Xinjiang, including setting up vocational education and training centers. Now safety and security has returned to Xinjiang and the fundamental human rights of people of all ethnic groups there are safeguarded."[41]

The vast majority of the fifty signatories represent countries and territories that stand to benefit from Belt and Road projects, and many depend particularly on trade transiting through Xinjiang. South and central Asian states like Pakistan, Tajikistan, Uzbekistan, and Turkmenistan, as well as Middle Eastern nations like Iran, Syria, Iraq, Kuwait, the UAE, and Saudi Arabia—all signatories to the resolution— rely in whole or in part on Xinjiang for integration into the Silk Road Economic Belt, a reality reflected in numerous public statements of overt support for China's project to reeducate the Uyghur people.[42]

More importantly for China, the economic incentive to self-censor trickled westward into European capitals. While parliaments in Britain, France, and the Czech Republic have labeled the atrocities in Xinjiang a genocide, other governments across Europe were hesitant to respond—and remain so at the time of this writing. Germany in particular has refrained from changing its trade relationship with China, even in the face of possible complicity in Uyghur forced labor schemes in Xinjiang.[43] Such is the behavior that Beijing seeks to inculcate and the community that Xi hopes to build: self-censoring governments that erode their own values and norms through their silence. Everyone has a price, and the CCP believes it has found Europe's bottom line: retaining market access to China. This complacency is fuel for the BRI and the prerequisite for uniting Eurasia on China's terms, even if it happens at the cost of a genocide.

FROM A CORK TO A HUB: THE BRI IN THE PACIFIC

September 2019 was an unfortunate month for Taiwan. In the span of one week, Taipei lost two Indo-Pacific allies to Beijing's overtures: the Solomon Islands and Kiribati. Both countries lie in the South Pacific, a few thousand miles off Australia's coast. Although far removed from Taiwan's shores, these islands were regional governments who up until then had given Taiwan what it badly needed: diplomatic validation of its distinct status from the PRC. In its ongoing quest to isolate Taipei and eventually bring the island-country under its governance, the CCP flipped the Solomon Islands and Kiribati not with coercion, but with inducements. Mere months after acceding to Beijing's "One-China principle" and affirming China's sovereignty claim over Taiwan, Kiribati signed a Memorandum of Understanding (MOU) with the PRC on Belt and Road projects.[44] Likewise, Beijing rewarded the Solomon Islands for its diplomatic about-face with a reported commitment of $500 million in financial aid, easily eclipsing Taiwan's economic assistance to Honiara.[45] But Xi's gambit in the South Pacific exceeded the isolation of Taiwan.

By 2021, Beijing's strategic intent became clear: upgrading a runway on Kiribati's island of Kanton. The runway was originally constructed in 1939 and utilized by the U.S. Army during World War II to accommodate heavy bombers. Eventually the runway fell into disuse and was reserved only for emergency landings. More than fifty years later, the CCP moved to resurrect the airstrip—as well as the geostrategic status of Kiribati. In the words of an unnamed adviser, "The island would be a fixed aircraft carrier" for the People's Liberation Army.[46] Although China was coy at the time, Kiribati's ambassador to the PRC eventually confirmed that the project was connected to the BRI.[47]

The situation was remarkably similar in the Solomon Islands. In March 2022, news broke of Honiara's decision to ink a policing cooperation initiative with Beijing. China had brokered similar arrangements with Papua New Guinea, Fiji, and Vanuatu. But the agreement with the Solomon Islands went further: a grant of port access for People's Liberation Army Navy (PLAN) vessels.[48] The Solomon Islands quickly disputed the possibility of China establishing a military base on their territory, but the denial was of little consolation to Washington and Canberra. Both capitals had heard similar protestations from the Cambodian government, only to see Beijing establish a military base there.[49]

The BRI works on dual time horizons in the Pacific Ocean for Beijing. In the short run, the CCP is angling to turn Taiwan from a cork into a hub. Given the island's position between Japan and the Philippines, Taiwan complicates the PLAN's ability to access the deep waters of the Pacific Ocean on ideal terms. According to Xi's calculus, each lost ally for Taiwan is another incremental step toward his ultimate goal of unifying Taiwan with the PRC. BRI projects offer a tempting inducement for Pacific Island countries to ditch Taipei for Beijing.

But restoring landing strips that could service PLA bombers and securing port access for Chinese surface warfighting vessels reveals ambitions that transcend Taiwan. The CCP is using the BRI to break open the Pacific Ocean for another reason: unencumbered power projection. The United States has dominated the Pacific since 1945; the PRC is angling to unseat America's military in the world's largest ocean. As far as China is concerned, Pacific Island countries are either with the Middle Kingdom or against it. For those who align with Beijing, lucrative contracts await. For those who resist, China knows how to up the ante. Whether weaponizing overfishing in the waters surrounding American Samoa[50] or leveraging tourism to cripple the economies of Palau and the Northern Marianas Islands,[51] China is seeking preponderance over the Pacific by hook or crook. Some politicians have risked their lives and lost their careers by opposing the BRI in their countries.[52] Beijing's message to these small islands is simple but chilling: join the CCP's community, or else.

STRING OF PEARLS: THE BRI IN THE INDIAN OCEAN

"India is . . . so important that without her the Empire could not continue to exist."[53] These words, spoken in 1909 by Britain's viceroy of India Lord Curzon, underscore an unflinching reality for aspiring imperial powers: the Eurasian subcontinent is key. Napoleon of France and Alexander I of Russia looked toward it with envy, for the colonization of India provided the strategic high ground necessary for Britain's ability to dominate much of the Eastern Hemisphere. The Crown's possession of India necessitated control of the Suez Canal, which led to the colonization of Egypt. It also demanded a presence in South Africa and Mauritius, a small island nation east of Madagascar. Britain's dominion also extended to the Persian Gulf and the Gulf of Adan, thus flanking the Arabian Peninsula. The British used India as a gateway into the Himalayas and, briefly, a springboard to Java and the prized Malacca Straits.

These possessions, from South Africa and Adan to Burma and Australia, silhouette the Indian Ocean, with India resting atop. For the British, that India was the "centre and secret of Imperial dominion [sic]" was equally true on land.[54] British officials credited their most prized colony with England's ability to project power and influence from Persia to Southeast Asia.

The staying power of India remains, especially now as an independent and sovereign nation. At the time of this writing, it is on track to become the world's most populous nation by 2023.[55] Its economic growth is robust, and on matters of geopolitics it increasingly, though not exclusively, aligns itself with the West.

For all these reasons, India's strength is a challenge to the CCP. Achieving *tianxia* in the twenty-first century requires Beijing to reckon with this nation with a civilizational heritage that rivals its own. Unlike Imperial Britain, however, the CCP lacks the capacity to subdue India as a possession. Moreover, New Delhi made its thoughts about the BRI clear from the start, when it publicly demurred from joining the project in 2017.[56] India's intransigence has not stopped the CCP from copying the playbook of the British Empire.

Beijing is running Britain's strategy in reverse. Instead of possessing India and working outward, China is working from

the outside in, securing political influence and establishing tributary relations along the Indian Ocean's ring. If colonizing India
is not an option, then Xi is all too happy with the slow process
of strategic strangulation. Security analysts often refer to China's strategy as creating a "string of pearls"—an apt analogy, and
one brought to life by Xi's foreign policy.[57] The Belt and Road
follows Lord Curzon's imperial blueprint, point for point.

- **The Malacca Straits.** Three of the top five BRI
  recipients are Indonesia, Malaysia, and Singapore.[58]
  It is no coincidence that these nations hug the
  Malacca Straits. Currently, the U.S. Navy polices
  these waters and regularly operates out of Singapore. The rationale of China's investments in this
  critical juncture exceeds its nine-dash line in the
  South China Sea: Beijing is using material incentives to erode America's localized dominance. The
  stronger China grows at the Malacca chokepoint,
  the more tenuous India's position becomes at its
  Andaman and Nicobar Islands. To be sure, eject-
  ing the United States is a far cry, but China would
  be content with contesting Washington's presence.
  Doing so could hamper the ability of the U.S. Fifth
  and Seventh Fleets to mobilize in a crisis scenario in
  the Indian Ocean.

- **The Himalayas.** Sandwiched between China and
  India in the Himalayan heights, the small states
  of Nepal and Bhutan are a microcosm of imperial Confucianism: economic capture when possible, blunt force when necessary. Beijing has courted
  Katmandu for years, viewing the small sliver of

a nation as a potential commercial hub in its BRI ambitions.[59] While projects have been slow to materialize, the PRC has leveraged its potential to blunt Washington's and New Delhi's overtures at key moments, including scuttling Nepal's partnership with the U.S. National Guard.[60] With Bhutan, China has no subtlety. Unlike Katmandu, Thimphu has not joined the Belt and Road and has refrained from attending PRC-hosted summits on account of India's concerns. In response to Bhutan's accommodation of India, as well as dissatisfaction with a two-hundred-year-old treaty with the British Empire, the Middle Kingdom has literally moved into Bhutan, establishing Chinese settlements more than a mile past the recognized border.[61]

- **The Middle East.** China has "expanded its strategic priorities in the Middle East," according to Ilan Berman of the American Foreign Policy Council.[62] What was originally an arms export market and an energy import market has morphed into an opportunity for Beijing to project economic dominance into a region long dominated by the United States. Thus far, the CCP has made no distinctions between Israel, Iran, or the Arab states; it will seek partnerships wherever its interests lead. Judging by its hefty investments in Egypt's Suez Canal and its $27 billion total of BRI projects in Saudi Arabia, the Arabian Peninsula matters as much to Beijing as it did to the British Empire.[63] As with the rest of the world, China's military follows its investments. News broke in late 2021 of a secret PRC military base in the UAE, a nightmare scenario for the United States. Dubai initially halted the project after severe pushback from Washington,[64] but construction appeared to resume in April 2023.[65] Around the same time, Beijing brokered a restoration of relations between Riyadh and Tehran, solidifying its stature as a regional player and complicating America's diplomatic efforts.[66]

- **Sub-Saharan Africa.** To the West, Africa may well be "the forgotten continent," but to China, it is the land of opportunity. Since 2013, Beijing has poured $165 billion of BRI infrastructure projects and investments into Africa, comfortably outpacing its footprint in the Middle East.[67] The weak governance and rampant corruption that make U.S. private investment untenably risky provide an open opportunity for the Middle Kingdom to establish an unrivaled presence. In one way, China is playing the long game in Africa, which is estimated to reach population parity with Asia over the next century. But Beijing's Africa bet is already paying off, as African countries regularly side with the PRC at the United Nations.[68] More fundamentally, Beijing's broader effort to realize a Community of Common Destiny for All Mankind resonates deeply with Africa's colonial history. As Joshua Eisenman of Notre Dame University put it to me in a conversation, China's history with victimization "creates a kind of kinship with the Global South, but in a leadership [role] at the same time," which positions Beijing to "lead the Global South out of the victimization and into a rejuvenation."[69] What does the CCP gain from the rejuvenation of Africa? A military base in Djibouti, at the strategic chokepoint connecting the Gulf of Aden with the Red Sea, and a possible base in Equatorial Guinea, which could position China's navy in the Atlantic Ocean.[70]

- **Pakistan and Burma.** If India was Imperial Britain's crown jewel, Pakistan is the BRI's poster child. Beijing has promised upwards of $70 billion focused chiefly on transit infrastructure running from Urumqi to Gwadar.[71] The PRC is funding similar projects in Burma, though at a smaller scale.[72] These land routes to the Indian Ocean provide China what it has lacked since its inception: access to the Indian Ocean. To be sure, deep water ports in Gwadar and Kyaukphyu provide Beijing with an alternative to the Malacca Straits for energy imports. But these routes also introduce an uncomfortable outlook for India. If these ports follow the path of China's BRI projects in the Pacific, PLAN vessels could one day dock—perhaps base—to India's west and east, thus flanking New Delhi and contesting its activity in the Indian Ocean.

Recall the famed Chinese admiral Zheng He, whom Xi Jinping praised as he announced the Maritime Silk Road in Jakarta. Indonesia was a key stopover for Zheng, but it was not his final destination. According to Chinese records, Zheng sailed beyond the South China Sea and made stops in the Bay of Bengal, the Arabian Sea, the Persian Gulf, the Arabian Peninsula, and the east coast of Africa. Diagrammed on a map, it becomes clear that one of the Ming dynasty's overriding objectives was to secure Chinese economic interests across the entirety of the Indian Ocean. According to Wan Ming of the Chinese Academy of Social Sciences, "People of the Ming had thus a clear realization that the Western Oceans and Western Regions were connected to each other."[73]

Overlaying Zheng He's voyages with Xi Jinping's Maritime Silk Road reveals a startling alignment between two ventures separated by six hundred years. This remarkable symmetry suggests the existence of an abiding interest for China in the Indian Ocean region, one that comes at the expense of New Delhi and Washington.

TO THE ENDS OF THE EARTH: THE BRI IN LATIN AMERICA

Many nations have tried to weaken the United States' dominance in the Western Hemisphere. During the Civil War, Napoleon III openly supported Southern secession and concurrently sought to establish a Francophile emperor in Mexico. In the run-up to World War I, Wilhelmine Germany played the Mexico card again and sought to turn America's southern neighbor against the Allies. Adolf Hitler turned his gaze farther South, and Argentina, Brazil, and Chile served as critical Nazi espionage hubs during World War II. The Soviets, of course, cultivated ties with Cuba to great effect.

As aspiring powers tried to dilute America's regional hegemony, Washington had a consistent advantage: its economic strength. Even before World War I, America was steadily displacing Britain as the primary trading partner with Latin American countries. This strength served as a backstop for American power in the face of external attempts to drive political and ideological wedges between the United States and its neighbors.

Now, of course, the situation is reversed. Beijing has unseated Washington as the region's primary economic partner, increasing trade with Latin American countries from $18 billion in 2002 to nearly $316 billion in 2019.[74] This trend is of great concern to Taiwan, as more than half of its remaining allies are in this region. As in the Pacific, Beijing is undoubtedly leveraging its wealth to isolate Taipei in the Western Hemisphere. Since 2007, Taiwan has lost Costa Rica, Panama, the Dominican Republic, El Salvador, Nicaragua, and Honduras to the PRC's overtures.[75]

But Xi's calculus goes beyond annexing Taiwan. From next-generation telecommunications infrastructure in Mexico and a strategic port in El Salvador to projects in the Caribbean and a space tracking facility in Argentina, the Belt and Road is ensconcing China's economic and strategic presence in the region. According to El Salvadorian president Nayib Bukele, the terms of BRI deals come "without conditions," a thinly veiled swipe at Washington's model of foreign assistance that demands governance and humanitarian standards.[76]

The U.S. military is well aware of the risks involved. According to Admiral Craig Faller, head of U.S. Southern Command, "As I look at where [China is] focused strategically—West Coast, East Coast, South Panama, Caribbean—I absolutely can see a future where these ports will become a hub for their growing blue water Navy that far exceeds their . . . need for homeland defense."[77]

Xi is leveraging China's economic might to achieve what Napoleon, the Kaiser, Hitler, and the Soviets sought: a weakened America in its near-abroad. Just like those regimes of old, the CCP has willing partners. Decades of authoritarian rule have effectively reduced Venezuela to a shell of a country.

"Venezuela," according to reporting in *Time*, "has experienced a slow-burn collapse of epic proportions, all while sitting atop the world's largest known oil reserves. Once the continent's largest economy, it can no longer feed its own people."[78] Hugo Chavez, Venezuela's strongman at the turn of the century, initially turned to the CCP, who gladly accepted Venezuelan crude at reduced prices in an oil-for-loan swap. Subsequently, the CCP and Nicolás Maduro, the current dictator in Caracas, have turned Venezuela into a test lab for high-tech authoritarianism. Thanks to PRC-controlled companies like Huawei, ZTE, and others, Caracas has surveillance-capable 5G networks and the "fatherland card," its Orwellian copy of the CCP's "social credit system" that incentivizes individual compliance and self-censorship.[79]

The CCP has served as a critical lifeline for the Cuban regime as well. When protests rocked the socialist dictatorship in July 2021, the regime in Havana quickly shut down the Internet and hamstrung the ability of democratic activists to coordinate and publicize their cause internationally. The nimbleness of the Cuban government's response was due to the censorship capabilities of its PRC-designed telecommunications network. Four months later, Cuba joined the BRI.[80]

In the case of Venezuela, Beijing—and Moscow, for that matter—has already begun using it as an extraterritorial hub for cyberattacks.[81] With Cuba, a future PLA military presence could present Washington with the same problems the U.S. military poses to the PRC in the South China Sea: the threat of shipping disruption in a crisis scenario.

In 1823, America warned European empires to stay out of its backyard. Today, Imperial China is ignoring this warning and violating Washington's Monroe Doctrine with its own version of Manifest Destiny. The Middle Kingdom's unbounded quest to rule all under heaven has brought it to America's doorstep—and, in the process, across the entire globe.

The Belt and Road Initiative is not Beijing's prelude to a future bid for superiority, but the expression of Beijing's present ambitions. The CCP is angling to realize them short of fighting, but the Middle Kingdom will stop at nothing to subjugate all under heaven and build a Community of Common Destiny for All Mankind. Imperial Confucianism lives on, and its success is nonnegotiable for the party.

THE WORLD IS DANGEROUS AGAIN

What, though, would such a world look like? For all the ways Beijing's influence and power are expanding, most Americans don't perceive any difference in their daily lives. That is a blessing to be cherished, for those unfortunate enough to live in the BRI's shadow know the cost of refusing to kowtow to China. I discovered this firsthand on April 26, 2023.

That Wednesday morning, I walked downstairs from my third floor office to AFPC's basement conference room for a meeting with Daniel Suidani, an erstwhile premier of Malaita, the largest province in the Solomon Islands. Suidani had lost his position in a no-confidence vote and was traveling through Washington for meetings with government officials and China hands to explain what happened. Typically, a low-level shakedown in a far-flung island nation halfway across the world wouldn't even register on DC's Richter scale. This one, though, was different.

Suidani lost his seat at the behest of a well-funded and focused campaign led by pro-CCP elements in the Solomon Islands and fronted by Manasseh Sogavare. Suidani had incited

Beijing's wrath by opposing Honiara's diplomatic switch from Taipei to Beijing four years prior.[82] In 2019, Suidani also imposed a moratorium on all investments with the CCP and tried to insulate his province of Malaita from Beijing's malign influence.[83] In 2022, Suidani turned more heads when he publicly criticized a bilateral security agreement between Honiara and Beijing. That same year, even as Huawei was building out 5G telecommunications infrastructure across the Solomon Islands, Suidani blocked the giant Chinese company from making inroads into Malaita.[84]

For Sogavare, Suidani's integrity complicated the deal he just brokered with Xi Jinping. The scale of BRI investments rolling into Honiara, and the political benefits they offered, were too enticing to risk. So, when Suidani came down with a severe health condition that required medical care abroad, the central government slow-walked his request for foreign travel. Chillingly, they insinuated that he would receive expedited approval in exchange for tempering his anti-CCP stance.[85] Suidani only got the medical care he needed thanks to the generosity of Taiwan.

In a small country like the Solomon Islands, Beijing's malign influence runs deeper than politics and economics. Those brave enough to take a stand pay a price. That was the weighty truth I learned that day. In America, politicians routinely buck the CCP. Governors and senators wear Beijing's sanctions and anger as a badge of honor—and rightly so. Standing up to tyranny is a noble endeavor, but Americans, by and large, never pay the price. Such is the benefit of living under the shelter of a superpower. Many in this world, however, do not enjoy protection from their government against the CCP's predations. In some cases, their authorities are willing accomplices.

According to analysis from AidData, a Virginia-based research lab, leaders who align with China reap a financial windfall. "On average," according to AidData executive director Bradley Parks, "a 10 percent increase in voting alignment with China in the UN General Assembly yields a 276 percent increase in aid and credit from Beijing."[86] Standing for freedom comes at a high cost.

If Americans want to know what a CCP-dominated world would look like, look no farther than Daniel Suidani. Bow to Beijing, or lose your job and your well-being: that is the choice a Community of Common Destiny for All Mankind would foist on billions of people around the world. Over time, the totalitarian reality of daily life within China would become the daily reality of much of the world. That is the end state of the BRI and its imperialist zeal.

The world of the 1990s is long gone. The "end of history" dream was always a myth, one that America's political elites foolishly believed. We have now awoken from this dream into a living nightmare. The United States must act with resolve to preserve our security and uphold our commitments to our allies and partners. Unfortunately, Washington's China policy lacks clarity. If anything, it is marked by internal contradictions and knee-jerk reactions. The world is dangerous again, and America is not ready.

CHAPTER 4

AMERICA'S TRIUMPHALIST HANGOVER

THE FIVE STAGES of grief are denial, anger, bargaining, depression, and acceptance. As odd as it may sound, America is unconsciously grieving the death of its unipolar moment, the brief interlude between America's Cold War victory and the terrorist attacks on September 11, 2001, when the United States existed, in the words of the American columnist Charles Krauthammer, as "the unchallenged superpower."[1] Today, unfortunately, the United States seems unable to move beyond stage two. When Vladimir Putin invaded and annexed Crimea, Ukraine's Black Sea peninsula, in 2014, Washington elites were aghast that any world leader would reject Western norms and revert to the supposedly archaic practice of offensive warfare. Then–secretary of state John Kerry was positively befuddled: "You just don't in the 21st century behave in 19th century fashion by invading another country on completely trumped up pretext. It is serious in terms of sort of the modern manner with which nations are going to resolve problems."[2] That word, "modern," tips his hand. Kerry was clinging to the belief that imperialism was dead, that warfare itself was abnormal in a liberal internationalist world. Just like followers of a religion, Kerry and his cohorts still held out hope for Russia's salvation: "There are all kinds of other options still available to Russia. There still are."[3] This was less of an olive branch for Putin and more of a cry for help on behalf of a disintegrating new world order.

To be sure, there were plenty clearer heads in Washington. Mike Rogers, then-chair of the House Intelligence Committee, admitted that Russia was "running circles around us."[4] The recommended solutions from many Russia hawks, however, fell short. Kicking Russia out of the G8 and slapping Moscow with sanctions were easy responses with minimal payoff, and they failed to alter Putin's calculus.[5] It was a failure of imagination and anticipation. Instead of preempting Putin's next moves and shaping his choices, foreign policy hawks were content to react and play defense. As it turns out, policymaking via press releases weakens national security.

These dual issues—denial and defensiveness—have also plagued America's China policy in recent years, and the results are nothing short of catastrophic: the United States is not behaving like a confident superpower in its reckoning with Beijing's imperialism. For its part, the Biden administration is seeking "coexistence" with the PRC by attempting to split the difference between cooperation and competition. Meanwhile, "China hawks" in Congress are advocating for reactionary measures to blunt Beijing's march toward global hegemony. Both approaches are misguided for different reasons. The doves are strengthening the CCP; the hawks are missing opportunities to counter it.

DEFENDING THE WRONG THING

On May 26, 2022, Secretary of State Antony Blinken announced the Biden administration's long-awaited China strategy. "Under President Xi," Blinken asserted, "the ruling Chinese Communist Party has become more repressive at home and more aggressive abroad." He went on to name the CCP's offenses: mass exportation of digital surveillance technology, violating international waters in the South China Sea, exploiting American companies, and oppressing its own people. The secretary was equally clear about the entity with the most to lose from the CCP's actions—the international order: "China is the only country with both the intent to reshape the international order and, increasingly, the economic, diplomatic, military, and technological power to do it."[6]

It is an odd thing for the chief diplomat of a sovereign nation-state to elevate the health of global institutions above the interests of his or her own government. Blinken couched his remarks not in terms of the United States' history as a great power, nor its ideological heritage from the eighteenth century, but in relation to the establishment of the United Nations and the Universal Declaration of Human Rights. Throughout his remarks, Blinken's references to the international order outnumbered his mentions of U.S. vital interests. The subtext was unmistakable: the Biden administration's top priority in its relationship with Beijing is perpetuating the "new world order" that George H. W. Bush heralded. Secretary Blinken is far from alone. President Biden insisted in his remarks at the United Nations in 2021, "All the major powers of the world have a duty, in my view, to carefully manage their relationships so they do not tip from responsible competition to conflict."[7]

To be sure, President Biden has taken a number of steps within the international system to shore up America's advantages against the CCP. His administration's investments in the quadrilateral security dialogue with Japan, India, and Australia are commendable, and his Indo-Pacific Economic Framework for Prosperity could potentially offer U.S. partners and allies economic alternatives to Beijing's overtures. Even so, liberal internationalism is naive triumphalism. It is a Pollyannaish miscalculation of how the world works: if nations forego the marginal gains they could accrue by competing in the short run, everyone enjoys larger returns in the long run. Or, as my old boss Senator Ted Cruz put it, "Put a daisy in the machine gun barrel, and the bad guys will suddenly like us."[8]

This outlook has led the Biden administration to downplay competition with the CCP in favor of cooperating with Beijing on multiple occasions:

+ In February 2021, Biden officials were unwilling to admit that the CCP's genocide of Uyghurs and other groups in Xinjiang was ongoing.[9]
+ That summer, Climate Envoy John Kerry worked to limit the number of Chinese companies that received an effective import ban for slave labor.[10]
+ In September, the Biden administration cut a deal with Huawei executive Meng Wanzhou and allowed her to return to China—a demand Chinese diplomats had officially registered with U.S. officials.[11]
+ In October, Deputy Secretary of State Wendy Sherman lobbied Congress against critical human rights legislation.[12] Administration officials subsequently

declined to sanction key Chinese entities after that bill became law.[13]

+ The following month, reports emerged of the State Department scrubbing the use of the phrase "malign actions" in its description of the CCP's behavior.[14]

+ In December, U.S. officials cut the video feed of Taiwan's digital minister during the Summit of Democracies for sharing a map that colored the PRC and Taiwan differently.[15]

+ In January 2022, American diplomats reportedly urged Lithuania to refrain from upgrading its de facto Taiwan embassy.[16]

+ In July 2022, President Biden sought to spike Speaker of the House Nancy Pelosi's planned trip to Taiwan to protect the cooperative momentum Washington and Beijing were building.[17]

+ In early 2023, the Biden administration allowed a PRC spy balloon to enter American airspace and sail across the continental United States. The administration initially sought to hide the balloon's existence from the public to protect diplomatic overtures with Beijing.[18]

+ Months later, senior State Department officials traveled to Beijing to run advance for Secretary Blinken's trip and landed in Beijing on June 4, the thirty-fourth anniversary of the Tiananmen Square massacre. The ill-timed arrival gifted a propaganda boon to the CCP.[19]

+ That same month, Secretary Blinken traveled to Beijing. A condition of his trip was not publicizing the FBI's report into Beijing's spy balloon.[20] To secure the visit, the State Department also froze human rights sanctions on Chinese officials and delayed export controls on Huawei.[21]

+ Throughout this time, no evidence exists of the Biden administration opening new investigations into U.S. universities that failed to report foreign gifts from the PRC. There is also little indication of official concern about Confucius Institutes, another issue about which PRC diplomats complained.[22]

Viewed in context, "responsible competition" seems deeply irresponsible. Remember, though, the orientation of liberal internationalism. The objective is not defeating adversaries but co-opting them into global institutions that supposedly transform them over time. Biden administration officials start from this reference point and insist that great power adversaries can coexist peacefully. For evidence, they turn—ironically—to the Cold War.

★★★★★

In 2021 Rush Doshi, Biden's China director at the National Security Council, published an impressive tome, *The Long Game: China's Grand Strategy to Displace American Order*. It is an exhaustive and measured articulation of the CCP's plans to unseat America as the global superpower. Yet, after three hundred pages of explaining the CCP's world-sized ambitions, Doshi throws a wrench into his own argument: "China is the necessary partner of the United States on virtually every transnational challenge from nonproliferation to climate change.... In the period ahead, the United States will need to delink [cooperation and competition] and hold fast to the rule that there will be two tracks in US-China ties: one focused on cooperation and one on competition."[23] According to the Biden administration's own track record, such a feat is easier said than done. But Doshi pointed to a time when America had apparently done this before: "The US and Soviet Union managed to collaborate in a far more existential competition than this one on a host of issues ranging from ozone to polio vaccination to space."[24] Looking at each example in turn, however, reveals a more complicated story.

Joint ozone efforts between Washington and Moscow, while impressive in their longevity, owed their success less to aligned political elites in Washington and Moscow and more to the issue's low political priority at the time. A 1988 academic study put it rather bluntly: "The environmental concerns do not involve strategic issues; there are no national security secrets to be divulged. . . . The low priority accorded the environmental exchanges may also have made them not worth canceling as a pawn in the political rivalries of these superpowers."[25] Today, however, the dynamic is categorically different. Biden places a high premium on climate policy, and China's diplomats have exploited it to the detriment of America's human rights agenda.

At first glance, the polio analogy is compelling. In the midst of an ongoing arms race, the scientific communities in America and the Soviet Union somehow found a way, with help from the World Health Organization, to join forces in vaccine research to blunt the polio epidemic. This ray of sunshine, however, only began to break through the clouds in the mid-1950s—more specifically, after the death of Joseph Stalin.[26] Beyond that, the Soviets were painfully aware of the ways

American science could help them combat polio. In the words of one historian, "It was costly socially and economically not to take advantage of the great breakthroughs in American biomedical research vis-à-vis polio."[27]

These conditions do not exist today. Unlike polio, the health crisis of our time, COVID-19, started because of America's great-power adversary. As we will examine later, the CCP initially concealed the virus' existence, then punished foreign governments that sought information about its origins.[28] Moreover, Xi has rebuffed American-developed vaccines and opted instead for Chinese-produced solutions.[29] Given its recent behavior, the Biden administration's assumption that the CCP could behave as a good-faith partner on public health policy strains credulity.

Finally, Doshi's claim of US-Soviet space cooperation is especially odd. In 2008, Roald Sagdeev, the head of the Russian Space Research Institute from 1973 to 1988, published his firsthand account of US-Soviet space cooperation—or lack thereof: "Both countries gave primary emphasis in their space efforts to a combination of national security and foreign policy objectives, turning space into an area of active competition for political and military advantage. . . . Only in the late 1980s, with warming political relations, did momentum for major space cooperation begin to build."[30]

This, of course, does not negate the rare moments of substantive collaboration between Washington and Moscow throughout the Cold War, particularly the Apollo-Soyuz Test Project docking mission in the 1970s and jointly photographing Halley's comet in the 1980s. But the Soviets regularly linked space cooperation with geopolitical concerns, from Khrushchev's demands for Eisenhower to remove forward-deployed nukes from Europe to Gorbachev's insistence that Reagan back off of missile defense investments. It wasn't until 1987, when Moscow formally dropped its linkage of space cooperation and arms control, that the two powers were able "to take steps toward actual cooperation."[31]

Great power cooperation didn't just "happen" during the Cold War. It was the product of conditions that do not exist between Washington and Beijing today. That is the failure of naive triumphalism: it presupposes an outcome—peace—that is often the result of the successful exercise of unilateral state power, the very thing the "new world order" seeks to limit and control.

HAWKS: REACTING INSTEAD OF ATTACKING

On December 3, 2020, the Trump administration announced an import ban on all cotton produced in Xinjiang, China's westernmost territory.[32] The issue at hand was the CCP's repression of Uyghur Muslims in Xinjiang, which included not only "reeducation" camps, but also forced labor. Xinjiang cotton accounts for roughly 20 percent of global supply.[33] Without even knowing it, Americans were financing the CCP's genocide by purchasing T-shirts, blouses, and socks.

The administration's import ban received wide bipartisan support from members of Congress, including Marsha Blackburn, a Republican senator from Tennessee. Early that morning, Blackburn publicly thanked Trump for his decision.[34] A few hours later, Blackburn had more to say: "China has a 5,000 year history of cheating and stealing. Some things will never change."[35]

CCP propagandists had a field day with Blackburn's commentary, using it not only to deflect from legitimate accusations of forced labor but also to claim that Republican China hawks were using China as a boogeyman for Trump's electoral defeat. Chen Weihua, the notorious *China Daily* bureau chief in Brussels, pointed to anti-Chinese rhetoric in the United States to justify Beijing's "wolf warrior diplomacy": "If such despicable words, deeds and conspiracies do not trigger the strongest response from Chinese diplomats, then they are not doing their job."[36]

The episode is a microcosm of the shortcomings of Washington's "pivot" on China policy, but not for the reasons most people think. True, Blackburn is only one of many American politicians who have judged the entirety of China's history by the CCP's actions. Doing so strengthens Beijing's hand and diverts focus away from the party's atrocities. But the real shame wasn't Blackburn's remarks; it was the reactive nature of China hawks writ large.

★★★★★

The relationship between the United States and the PRC changed more in 2020 than in the past four decades. China's initial concealing of the SARS-COV-2 virus's existence and subsequent stonewalling of information sharing, its attempts to profit off stockpiled personal protective equipment, and its blatant disinformation campaigns about the virus's origin all fed a retributive zeitgeist to "make China pay" for its culpability in the COVID-19 pandemic. This impulse, while understandable, caused U.S. policymakers to fixate on Beijing's past behavior instead of shaping the CCP's future choices. Bad ideas immediately defined the policy debate and hamstrung America's new approach to China.

Consider the push in 2020 to strip China of sovereign immunity in U.S. courts.[37] Allowing Americans to sue the PRC for pandemic damages is a quintessentially populist and woefully unserious idea. Doing so would require new legislation from Congress that would almost certainly garner a challenge at the Supreme Court. The reason is simple: it would upend centuries of international law and, quite possibly, the concepts of foreign direct investment and multinational corporations.

In some cases, these bad ideas also sabotaged good efforts. Take "decoupling" and "de-risking," recent buzzwords among China hands. While Washington has tried—with good reason—to reorient supply chains away from China, some members of Congress also called for the United States to leave the World Trade Organization, a move that then-president Donald Trump supported.[38] These initiatives contradict each other. The former sought to decouple the international trading system from China, while the latter policy would have decoupled the United States from global commercial institutions. Taken in isolation, reshaping supply chains has a great deal of merit, and Congress has begun legislating on these efforts with the support of the Biden administration.[39] But walking away from free trade writ large would harm the economic prospects of the American people and hurt our partners.

This reactive posture is not confined to COVID-19 politics. Washington has threatened to delist PRC companies from U.S. securities exchanges, prosecuted intellectual property theft, sanctioned human rights violators, and—to come full circle—banned tainted imports from China. These initiatives are worthy endeavors, even necessary ones, and the political leaders pushing them deserve credit for rejecting the naive triumphalist belief that engaging China economically would change China politically. Even so, no offensive strategy ties these confrontational ideas together. It is natural for America to address the accumulated problems of engaging the CCP for four decades, but we cannot "edit-undo" our way to outcompeting Beijing. We need to create problems for the party—something Washington has been slow to do. To understand why, we turn to the end of, yet again, the Cold War.

★★★★★

The United States is one of few nations in human history that can legitimately claim superpower status. Americans are accustomed to comparisons with ancient Egypt, Greece, and Rome—the very architecture of Washington, DC, draws parallels to these ancient empires. But America is arguably in a class of its own. Egypt, Greece, and Rome were regional powers with impressive but limited reach. Even the European empires, for all their far-flung colonies, constantly competed with each other and never established lasting primacy. In 1991, however, America sat atop the global power hierarchy as the world's undisputed—and perhaps history's only—"hyperpower." This status, while enviable, has actually corroded the ability of policymakers to think proactively about national security.

Grand strategy in the United States is generally taught and practiced as a rote three-step process: define interests, identify threats to those interests, and mobilize resources to defend interests and mitigate threats. This approach has conditioned the United States to be highly reactive, jumping from one crisis to the next. To a degree, this is unavoidable for a hegemon: by definition, an undisputed superpower has everything to lose and little left to gain. Thus, the strategic flow begins with risk instead of reward. Once you're the king of the hill, there's nowhere to go but down.

Conversely, aspiring global powers tend to approach strategy from a different starting point: relatively little to lose, and much to gain. In most cases, force-on-force comparisons are simply unfeasible against a hyperpower, so revisionists like the CCP naturally look for asymmetric vulnerabilities in their adversaries. Beijing's construction of artificial atolls throughout the South China Sea encapsulates this indirect approach: salami-slicing its way into its neighbors' exclusive economic zones and establishing facts on the ground that Vietnam, the Philippines, and others are unable to challenge. By the time the Pentagon raised the issue and Congress sounded the alarm, it was too late.[40] This was by design. Instead of looking at strategy through a defensive prism, the CCP is competing creatively and offensively, beginning the strategic process through the prism of exploiting the hegemon's weaknesses.

This perspective is woefully underappreciated in Washington today. Hawks regularly talk about *why* America and China are at odds—namely, antipodal ideologies. Lost in this discussion is the equally important question of *how* Washington is competing with Beijing. The ideological dimension of this contemporary Cold War is real, but overemphasizing its importance skews reality. In my five years as a foreign policy staffer in the U.S. Senate, I lost count of the number of times members on the Armed Services Committee and Foreign Relations Committee said the following: "America's greatest comparative advantage is its alliances. China doesn't have any allies." True, the CCP has no security relationships that are comparable to the alliance architecture the United States has built since

World War II. But that observation misses this point entirely. China has never leveraged its foreign policy to build an egalitarian world. The CCP is one of several Chinese dynasties that measures success not by its number of friends but by its tributary total. Having ignored this reality for decades, our national muscles have atrophied. For all the vestiges of strength, America is two steps behind Beijing.

A wholesale repudiation of the "end of history" creed is necessary, but unmitigated hawkishness cannot undo this damage. Foolish triumphalism predisposed Washington to be reactionary, even lazy, after the Cold War's dissolution. Today, as America once again reenters an era of great power competition, we need to accept this reality. But we need to do more than sober up. The bill for America's strategic lethargy has come due. The cost of defaulting on this payment is high. The moment compels us to change the way we think about security, and to practice strategy differently. Nothing short of these tectonic changes will increase America's chances of thwarting the Middle Kingdom's designs. Unfortunately, when it comes to the party's imperial ambitions expressed in the BRI, Washington is failing this test.

BUYING THE BRI: BUYING TIME FOR BEIJING

In 2018, Congress passed the Better Utilization of Investments Leading to Development (BUILD) Act, a public-private partnership to compete dollar for dollar with the Belt and Road Initiative.[41] The plan was to supersize America's Overseas Private Investment Corporation, rebrand it as the Development Finance Corporation (DFC), and grease the skids for U.S. companies to enter risky foreign markets. While the word "China" didn't appear in the legislation, representatives and senators were explicit about the act's purpose. According to Senator Chris Coons from Delaware, the Build Act would position America to "compete with Chinese influence in the developing world."[42] The following year, the Trump administration announced plans to pool resources with Japan and Australia via the Blue Dot Network, a trilateral mechanism to fund these projects and also to rate the quality of Chinese loans.[43] Both objectives are commendable, and the United States has met with some success in steering nations like Burma away from BRI loans.[44]

Even so, the BUILD Act and Blue Dot Network represent slightly different methods of whack-a-mole, merely reacting to discrete Belt and Road projects whenever or wherever they arise. True, they are useful tools with which to arm American companies with more information about foreign markets, but it is unclear whether this transparency has solved the underlying problem for American companies: the market risk of investing in an economy with poor governance, low transparency, and corruption concerns. None of these red flags are issues for Chinese state-owned enterprises, but private American firms are legally bound to consider them.

In 2022 the Organization for Economic Cooperation and Development (OECD) published its plan to square this circle. "By raising awareness and promoting international standards among low- and middle-income countries," the report claimed, "a Blue Dot Network certification may encourage them to implement reforms of their governance systems or regulatory frameworks."[45] This approach may work for social media companies where millions of users seek coveted verification, but it is unclear how many nations in the Global South actually want "blue dots" from the West. If anything, recent polling across the Middle East and Africa suggests that China's popularity is eclipsing America's.[46] Washington politicians can warn about "Chinese debt traps" all they want, but actual projects from Beijing—for all their drawbacks—are better than theoretical investment from America.

To its credit, the Biden administration has worked to address this problem. In June 2021, the White House announced the Build Back Better World (B3W) initiative, a G7 project that aimed to "collectively catalyze hundreds of billions of dollars of infrastructure investment for low- and middle-income countries in the coming years."[47] The administration wasn't shy about B3W's purpose: "The United States is rallying the world's democracies to deliver for our people, meet the world's biggest challenges, and demonstrate our shared values."[48] A year later, however, the White House rebranded the entire project, as the president's Build Back Better domestic initiative languished in Congress.[49] Perhaps, the thinking went, naming America's response to the BRI after a failed project at home was suboptimal messaging.

Perhaps—but not nearly as suboptimal as the projects the United States was financing. Senator Jim Risch (R-ID), the ranking member on the Senate Foreign Relations Committee, raised concerns in late 2021 about the Development Finance Corporation's clean energy investments. According to a publicized letter Risch sent the DFC, eighteen out of twenty-one DFC solar projects sourced solar panels from the PRC.[50] The American entity tasked with countering the BRI was funding projects that utilized the slave labor of religious minorities within China's BRI commercial hub. "Suboptimal" may be too kind a word to describe this self-defeating policy.

Even when the DFC manages to avoid boosting PRC companies, its reliance on the private sector places a concrete ceiling on its ability to go toe to toe with Chinese state-owned enterprises. In a private conversation at the American Foreign Policy Council (AFPC), diplomats from a central Asian nation shared their frustration with the DFC's inability to offer competitive interest rates. In one case, the government in question was deciding between a 14 percent offer from DFC and a 3 percent offer from Beijing.[51] That spread leaves foreign governments without a true choice, even if they would prefer to decrease their reliance on the CCP.

Both Republicans and Democrats appear to be doubling down on mistakes. Over the past few years, America's response to the BRI has shown itself to be an unholy alliance of naive triumphalism and knee-jerk hawkism. Whereas the progressive belief in transnational cooperation leads Democrats to inadvertently fund ethically tainted Chinese solar panels, reflexive confrontation compelled many Republicans to vote for the DFC and simply throw money at American companies—a poor response to the bottomless coffers of Chinese national champions. Neither response is serious, and both are doomed to fail.

Lurking underneath the surface of these embarrassing failures is a lack of vision. As my AFPC colleague and disinformation expert Ilan Berman put it, "We are increasingly not exactly sure what we're telling the world about America, and about why they should back the United States. . . . We don't know what we're saying in the context of great power competition. We have not woven a compelling narrative that would get global publics to back us and not back the Chinese."[52] Our hopes for building a "modern" China turned out to be built on sand, and we are adrift without a shared, coherent story to believe in and to share. America doesn't need counterprograming propaganda to drown out Beijing's noise. We need to speak with renewed inner clarity about America's strengths and the CCP's weaknesses. After all, our struggle against the CCP, according to Berman, is "not just a resource competition, it's not just a tech competition—it's a values clash. It's a systems clash. And this systems clash is something that the Chinese are actively selling."[53]

Washington needs to look past one-off infrastructure investments, recognize China's larger gambit with the BRI, and target the initiative's macrostructure. Doing so will require policymakers to dust off decades-old strategic tools that once served America well but have since fallen into disrepair. We must rediscover why we won the first cold war, if we are to win the one we are currently fighting.

Let us, then, be specific about what we need. Capitol Hill has a surplus of China-focused legislation but a deficit of truly competitive policies. Washington has an abundance of China hawks, but they are fixated on yesterday's problems. America needs specific ideas predicated on Beijing's weaknesses that policymakers can test. We must—as our grandfathers and grandmothers did in the prior cold war—redirect our adversary's investments, deter its adventurism, and move the competition to terrain on which it cannot fight. The more we operate within this paradigm, the more difficult it will be for Xi Jinping to invade Taiwan, expand the BRI, and lock in his vision for a "Community of Common Destiny."

LESSONS OF COLD WAR

During the Cold War, the existential stakes of protracted competition with the Soviet Union—namely, the specter of nuclear Armageddon—forced the United States to practice strategy like its life depended on it. Practically, this meant rejecting a top-down approach to strategy and, effectively, learning how to compete once again like a hungry young power. Instead of adopting a defensive posture, U.S. strategists honed the craft of identifying America's asymmetric strengths and exploiting the Soviet Union's strategic weaknesses.

This process took decades to perfect, largely because relearning the art of strategy is difficult enough for one person, let alone an entire bureaucracy and political elite. Andrew Marshall, the venerable Cold War strategist, summarized this challenge in 1990: "The process of justifying expenditures as counters to Soviet expenditures conditioned U.S. actions on Soviet strengths, expressed as threats, not on Soviet weaknesses and constraints. We had a war strategy—a catastrophic spasm—but no plan about how to compete with the Soviet Union over the long term."[54] That catastrophic spasm is once again evident in America's response to the CCP. But, thanks to Marshall and the Pentagon's Office of Net Assessment (ONA), which he led for many years, Washington now has a blueprint to follow: net assessment and competitive strategy. President Bush didn't mention these concepts in his triumphalist remarks in 1990, but containment would have been a clanging gong or a resounding cymbal without them.

Net assessments identify an adversary's vulnerabilities. Competitive strategies exploit them. According to Marshall, three questions guide this process:

1. What game is the United States playing?
2. What game is our adversary playing?
3. What are their relative strengths and weaknesses?[55]

During the latter half of the Cold War, this framework empowered policymakers to move past détente and actually compete with the Soviet Union by capitalizing on America's unique advantages over the Soviets—namely, the United States' free political system, market economy, and technological edge. In other words, the United States practiced strategy as a bottom-up exercise, not only as a top-down endeavor.

What did this look like practically, though? How did America seize the initiative from the Soviets and put Moscow on its heels? Three successful episodes are worthy of brief study and imitation: air defense, nuclear targeting, and defense spending.

In the late 1970s, Marshall and ONA examined the various legs of America's nuclear triad, which still to this day consists of land-based intercontinental ballistic missiles (ICBMs), submarine-launched ballistic missiles (SLBMs), and heavy bombers. Whether from land, sea, or sky, Washington and Moscow had multiple ways to annihilate each other. Marshall noted Joseph Stalin's strange obsession with heavy bombers, which stemmed from the USSR's fear of America's firebombing runs targeting Nazi Germany and Imperial Japan during World War II. This history, coupled with America's regular reconnaissance overflights of Soviet territory, predisposed Moscow to invest heavily in air defense. The Pentagon tested this hypothesis with the B-1 bomber. It wasn't even slated for production until 1982, but "the concept of a low-flying supersonic bomber played to Soviet fears," explains London School of Economics visiting professor Gordon Barrass, "and the Soviet air defense forces leaped to the bait. The Soviets spent billions on developing the MiG025, new surface-to-air missiles, and radar to counter this threat."[56] From Marshall's perspective, every ruble spent on defense was one less ruble available for first-strike nuclear weapons.

Military technology is one thing; political decision-making is another. Even if we scrambled the Soviet's investments,

America still needed to address the amorphous issue of perception. Were we successfully persuading the elites in Moscow that the cost of fighting a nuclear war outweighed the benefits of winning one? In the final years of the Carter administration, the United States sent an unmistakable message to the Kremlin: we know where your secret bunkers are, and our missiles can reach each of them. Carter approved the deployment of two hundred MX missiles (each with multiple nuclear warheads) in secret bunkers throughout America and also signaled Washington's intent to deploy Pershing II intermediate-range missiles in Europe in the coming years if Moscow didn't agree to arms control measures.[57] Especially clever were selective leaks from Presidential Directive 59 in July 1980, which outlined Carter's decision to target Soviet command and control centers if the USSR attacked the United States first.[58] Too many leaders in Washington today have forgotten the stabilizing effect of prudent brinkmanship.

It wasn't until the 1980s, however, that America gained an irreversible advantage over the Soviet Union. After his landslide victory and inauguration in 1981, Ronald Reagan indicated his belief that the time was ripe for delivering a death blow to the regime in Moscow:

> I learned the Soviet economy was in even worse shape than I'd realized [during the 1980 presidential campaign]. I had always believed that, as an economic system, Communism was doomed.... Now, the economic statistics and intelligence reports I was getting during my daily National Security Council briefings were revealing tangible evidence that Communism as we knew it was approaching the brink of collapse, not only in the Soviet Union but

> throughout the Eastern bloc. . . . You had to wonder how
> long the Soviets could keep their empire intact. If they
> didn't make some changes, it seemed clear to me that in
> time Communism would collapse on its own weight, and
> I wondered how we as a nation could use these cracks in
> the Soviet system to accelerate the process of collapse.[59]

This excerpt from President Reagan's autobiography is a
prime example of a net assessment: identifying a weakness in
your adversary ripe for exploitation. Washington had something Moscow lacked: a strong economy. Reagan leveraged that
advantage with devastating effect. From fiscal year (FY) 1980
to FY1985, America's defense spending increased by nearly
50 percent.[60] The Pentagon also outpaced the Soviets tech-
nologically, particularly with the development of the Strategic Defense Initiative, Reagan's gambit for space-based missile
defense. The program was young and had years of development to go, but the United States successfully duped Moscow
into thinking otherwise.[61] By 1986, the Soviet economy was
sputtering, and Moscow couldn't keep up with the competitive
pace America set.

To be sure, the United States still responded to Soviet
movements and stratagems throughout the Cold War, just as
the Soviets responded to American decisions. But the reaction
was tied to a larger competitive rubric. Caught in an existential death match with the Soviets, policymakers in Washington
had no choice but to compete on dual planes that simultaneously defended their core interests while also understanding—
and sabotaging—Moscow's game. Instead of thrashing about,
the United States acted deliberately, baiting the Kremlin into
decisions that favored Washington's strengths.

COMPETING TO WIN

Today, however, it is China that is baiting America, and the BRI is a textbook example. Washington's instinctual response to compete with the Belt and Road dollar for dollar is a losing proposition that plays into China's long game. But with an offensive framework, American policymakers could turn the tables and transform the BRI into an albatross to hang around the neck of the Communist Party. In many ways, net assessments and competitive strategies will be more difficult in this second cold war than they were in the first, for America's competition with the CCP is not just military in nature but also economic, political, and technological. The Belt and Road, for that matter, is also multidimensional, and as such is a complicated venture to target. As we will see, though, the massive project has multiple flanks that Washington has so far left untouched. The BRI is intrinsically connected to the systemic human rights abuses of Uyghur Muslims in Xinjiang because half of its land routes run through the territory and over the backs of oppressed minorities. Economically, meanwhile, the Belt and Road relies on corruption—and, in large part, the U.S. dollar—to grease the skids of construction. Militarily, its global scope could quickly overextend the PLA.

Each of these openings stems from weaknesses that are particular to the PRC and its ruling Communist Party. China has adeptly exploited America's strategic complacency, but China's brittle political system, totalitarian ideology, and fear of its own people all serve to complicate the BRI. The entire plan has multiple weaknesses at key nodes that, if pushed, could jeopardize the entire project. By harnessing the tools of net assessment and competitive strategies, U.S. policymakers could initiate targeted campaigns to exploit these vulnerabilities, atrocities, and illicit activities and counter China's "great game" one step at a time.

CHAPTER 5

BLUNTING BEIJING'S EMPIRE

THREE YEARS BEFORE al-Qaeda attacked America on September 11, 2001, Osama bin Laden told the world exactly what he thought of the United States. Unlike the Soviets, who brawled with the mujahideen in Afghanistan for more than twenty years, the Americans were a "paper tiger." Fresh in his mind were the Somali civil war and America's disastrous operations in the "Black Hawk Down incident" at Mogadishu. What was supposed to be a pinprick special forces mission to capture a warlord turned to chaos as Somali fighters shot down three American Black Hawk helicopters. In the wake of eighteen fatalities and eighty-four injuries, the U.S. military folded and withdrew from Somalia in 1995—merely three years after arriving. In 1998, bin Laden took the measure of the United States and found it wanting: "America assumed the titles of world leader and master of the New World Order. After a few blows, it forgot all about those titles and rushed out of Somalia in shame and disgrace, dragging the bodies of its soldiers. America stopped calling itself world leader and master of the New World Order, and its politicians realized that those titles were too big for them and that they were unworthy of them."[1] He then shifted from critiquing to warning, "The American government is leading the country towards hell."

In 2001, al-Qaeda followed through on that warning by raining down hellfire in New York and Washington, DC. Hijacked commercial airliners morphed into missiles and crashed into the World Trade Center and the Pentagon, America's symbols of economic and military dominance. Bin Laden wagered that the United States would retreat from the Middle East just as it had withdrawn from Somalia. Instead, the United States shook the world by invading Afghanistan and Iraq, overthrowing both regimes, and instituting democracies in the heart of the region. President George W. Bush clarified America's intent during his second inaugural address in 2005: "The survival of liberty in our land increasingly depends on the success of liberty in other lands. The best hope for peace in our world is the expansion of freedom in all the world. . . . So it is the policy of the United States to seek and support the growth of democratic movements and institutions in every nation and culture, with the ultimate goal of ending tyranny in our world."[2]

In a sense, America proved bin Laden wrong. Instead of cutting and running, Washington lurched in the opposite direction and hit the Taliban and Saddam Hussein like a wrecking ball. Of course, the plan was never to spend two decades rebuilding Afghanistan and Iraq. Despite Bush's lofty rhetoric, the DC establishment initially envisioned quick, decisive operations in both nations followed promptly by an organically funded rebuild.

Today, two decades later, this naivete conjures a half smile, a soft chuckle, and "a nod of comprehension beyond the laughter," as the theologian Reinhold Niebuhr once put it.[3] For not only is tyranny still very much with us, but America spectacularly failed to establish its new world order in the Middle East. This was due in no small part to bin Laden's adjusted strategy. If al-Qaeda and its affiliates could not bully America into leaving the Middle East, perhaps they could slowly bleed Washington over time. "All that we have to do," bin Laden explained in 2004, "is to send two mujahedeen to the furthest point east to raise a piece of cloth on which is written al Qaeda, in order to make generals race there to cause America to suffer human, economic and political losses without their achieving anything of note other than some benefits for their private corporations."[4] This "provoke and bait" strategy proved highly effective both operationally and financially. It cost al-Qaeda roughly $500,000 to carry out the 9/11 attacks.[5] The cost of America's quixotic campaign to "end tyranny in our world"? Eight trillion dollars—with precious little to show for it.[6] At the time of this writing, an Iran-friendly Shia government rules Iraq, and the Taliban, which provided safe haven to bin Laden and al-Qaeda, once again presides in Kabul.

Of course, the wars and reconstruction in Iraq and Afghanistan devolved into further challenges—namely, the rise of the Islamic State of Iraq and Syria, not to mention Bashar al-Assad's use of chemical weapons in the Syrian civil war. Next door, the mullahs in Tehran were accelerating their push to acquire nuclear weapons. To the northwest, Putin seized Crimea. The list of challenges was long, and America's capacity strained.

Around this time, as Princeton professor Aaron Friedberg has documented, leading PRC academics began to believe that

the United States had peaked as a great power. During the
Pentagon's 2007 "surge" in Iraq, leading PRC academics began
to believe the United States had "fallen into a fearful predicament" and that the "task of pacifying Iraq" was overextend-
ing Washington.[7] The War on Terror, according to Professor
Shi Yinhong of Renmin University, had imposed "a major
long-lasting constraint on US resources, energy, and attention."[8] In 2008, a PLA–affiliated journal argued that America had "no energy left to formulate a new strategy to deal
with China's rise. . . . Simply put, the United States has begun
to enter a period of relative decline."[9] In 2009, *People's Daily
Online* doubled down: "U.S. strength is declining at a speed so
fantastic that it is far beyond anticipation . . . the process of
multipolarization has been accelerated."[10] This belief went all
the way to the top. That same year, then–general secretary Hu
Jintao declared the need to "strengthen our strategic planning"
and "make more offensive moves."[11]

In Beijing's defense, America's own economic excesses supported this conclusion. Just one year after the surging of thousands of additional troops into Iraq, the U.S. housing market
collapsed. As global liquidity dried up, many nations that
had relied on debt-fueled growth suddenly found themselves
over-leveraged with scant ability to service their interest pay-
ments. This contagion came to a head in 2011, when the Euro-
zone was on the brink of collapse. At the G20 summit that year,
European leaders were looking for a savior. Notably, they were
not awaiting the arrival of Barack Obama, but of Hu Jintao. As
the *New York Times* put it, "The two contrasting appearances
at the Group of 20 economic meeting are a stark example of
waning American influence" that presaged "the relative decline
of the United States as an international force."[12]

This assumption was foundational to Xi's gambit with the BRI and his broader foreign policy: buying political influence with economic favors to displace the United States. As we have already seen, Beijing certainly had its own internal motives to launch the BRI—namely excess capacity, decreased economic growth, and the need to create more jobs. The project was a calculated risk—one that could only pay off if America remained distracted and diverted its focus to other problems. At the BRI's outset, the "propensity of things" certainly favored Beijing. America was fixated on the Middle East and Eastern Europe. Seemingly nothing stood in the CCP's way.

★★★★★

Does Xi have a lock on the project of the century? It is a matter of record that the BRI remains a work in progress, with many corridors incomplete and several projects under construction. But, from what we know now, will the CCP's gambit to usher in a Community of Common Destiny for All Mankind work?

Some analysts have seen enough. Tom Miller, author of *China's Asian Dream*, said he believes "the US needs to reach a tacit accommodation with Beijing" due to "the inevitability of China's rise."[13] Eyck Freymann, a Harvard-published scholar in East Asian studies, agrees: "There is also no guarantee that the West could stop [BRI] expansion even if it tried."[14] Others, like Bruno Maçães, foresee a disjointed world where the BRI "may never become universal . . . but in some areas it will rule unimpeded and different shades of influence will be felt everywhere."[15]

Others are far from convinced. Jonathan Hillman, an expert at the Center for Strategic and International Studies, sees the BRI not merely as an imperial grand strategy but more fundamentally as a frayed tapestry of incomplete projects with an uncertain outcome. As he argues in his cleverly titled book *The Emperor's New Road: China and the Project of the Century*, the BRI "is not a story about China's domination but its education as a rising power."[16] Given the Chinese economy's declining growth rate, the depletion of Beijing's foreign currency reserves, and the coronavirus that resulted in COVID-19, Hillman speculates that "Xi may be overreaching."[17]

Nobody knows the fate of twenty-first-century imperial Confucianism—not even Xi Jinping. That's what makes it difficult to accurately assess the BRI's actual threat to the United States. Conceptually, the entire project challenges American power and influence and purports to replace the U.S.-backed order with a Pax Sinica. Realistically, the BRI not only remains a work in progress but also has potential to morph into a liability for Beijing. China's slowing economic growth, the tenuous financial circumstances of several BRI partners, and the increasingly fraught bilateral relationship all pose enormous challenges to the realization of the "China Dream."

These sources of weakness, however, are not unique to the BRI or modern China. The Middle Kingdom has a way of falling into traps of its own making. Understanding the causes of China's past imperial failures shines much-needed light on the soft underbelly of the Belt and Road today.

OVEREXTENDED AND BLEEDING OUT: THE PITFALLS OF IMPERIAL CONFUCIANISM

China's imperial history defies oversimplification. The vastness of this era humbles the United States in its infancy and complicates the efforts of American strategists to understand the ebb and flow of China's history. Recall, though, China's ultimate aim: eliminating any gap between the Middle Kingdom's cultural greatness and its political authority. Aligning *zhongguo* and *tianxia* hinges on two requirements: unifying China, and expanding its dominion beyond its borders.

To be sure, this impulse—backed by a universally respected civilization and an unrivaled culture—armed China with energy and initiative in foreign affairs. It also, however, predisposed the Middle Kingdom to domestic stress and foreign overextension. When the son of heaven's territorial ambition exceeded his grasp, he jeopardized the Mandate of Heaven. Xi, and the CCP writ large, are predisposed to making these same mistakes today.

Parable 1: Domestic Stress

The Sui dynasty, which reigned from AD 581–618, is remembered for uniting northern and southern China in the wake of hundreds of years of disunion. Indeed, the Sui dynasty's claim to fame is much like the Qin's: they both brought order out of chaos and united the Middle Kingdom.

The Sui dynasty's ultimate fate, however, also mirrored the Qin's demise. The cost of binding China together was high and was paid for by the Chinese people themselves in the form of heavy taxation and forced labor for the Grand Canal, a series of massive projects to improve connectivity and transportation within China.[18] Ultimately, the Sui dynasty paid the price. Shortly after workers completed the early phase of Grand Canal construction, Emperor Yang conscripted well over a million soldiers for a series of ill-fated invasions of Korea. From AD 612–14, China invaded Korea three times and suffered defeat on each occasion.[19] The next year, the northern Xiongnu tribes humiliated Sui fighters and nearly captured emperor Yang in AD 617.[20] The Chinese people were weak from over-taxation, while the Middle Kingdom itself was exposed with losing campaigns on multiple fronts. The Kingdom of Sui lasted a mere twenty years.

Parable 2: Foreign Overextension

Successful Chinese dynasties are measured in hundreds of years, not tens. And hundreds of years before the Sui dynasty rose and fell, the Han dynasty was the pinnacle of success. After picking up the pieces of the Qin's downfall, the House of Han maintained control of China proper while expanding its territorial claims through conquest and colonization. The dynasty sought, in the words of Michael Schuman, "to match ideology with reality"—or *tianxia* with *zhongguo*—in the form of the tribute system.[21]

Over time, however, the economics of imperial Confucianism broke the bank. Perhaps counterintuitively, the tribute system was more expensive for Chinese dynasties than for the actual governments paying tribute. By its very nature, the Middle Kingdom gave more than it got from interactions with other nations. Over time, this imbalance resulted in a "courtly trade deficit," according to Schuman.[22] When the economy was growing, the cost was manageable. In leaner years, the Han dynasty resorted to suspending or limiting incoming tribute missions to spare its own coffers, as the dynasty did with the "Western Regions" (modern-day Xinjiang) in the early second century AD. The dilemma was a catch-22 for China. In the words of one Han courtier, "To meet [tribute demands] is beyond our means, but to reject them will surely cause alienation."[23]

The Han dynasty tried to keep these colonies on the cheap, with military outposts to keep the locals in line and their interests secured. This worked for a time, but at great cost of manpower and resources. Unfortunately, the targeted unwinding of the tribute system was emblematic of systemic weaknesses that metastasized a century later when the dynasty eventually collapsed under the burden of popular revolts over taxation and political jockeying over succession.

★★★★★

These two parables present two separate pitfalls for the CCP today. To be sure, they could happen at once, as they did for the Tang dynasty in AD 755.[24] For modern China, this history casts a grim light on the present. The PRC is just over seventy years old. It has surpassed the length of the Qin and the Sui dynasties but is nowhere near the longevity of the Han (nearly two hundred years) or Tang (nearly three hundred years). In a sense, the PRC's strategic future mirrors its economic challenges. Economists regularly speculate about China's odds of evading the "middle income trap" and establishing a wealthy middle class before its aging demographics preclude that possibility. The CCP's global ambitions depend in large part on making this transition; otherwise, the party could find itself in a "middle power trap" where China neither disappears as a mover and shaker in the world nor locks in regional hegemony in the Indo-Pacific, let alone the world.[25]

U.S. strategists can take no small degree of comfort in this perspective. True, China is a centuries-old entity that outshines America's relatively short existence—but the PRC is far younger than the United States, and its history is riddled with dynasties that failed to match the Middle Kingdom's political domain with its civilizational superiority. Even more concerning for Xi Jinping, China today faces economic stressors from within, a mixed BRI record marked with increasing cases of sovereign debt, and declining public opinion globally. The path ahead is perilous for the Belt and Road.

TIGHTENING BELT AND DANGEROUS ROAD

Much like the citizens of the Sui dynasty, the people of China are living under increasing economic strain. The days of sustained economic growth increasingly appear to be a relic of the past. Going into 2022, the CCP set a growth target of 5.5 percent for the year, yet the economy only grew by 0.4 percent in the second quarter.[26] Given the penchant for CCP apparatchiks to cook the books for their own benefit, the actual figure could be far worse. The party's recent "zero-COVID" policy has undoubtedly slashed economic growth across the country, but this new normal predates the pandemic. It stems primarily from Beijing's unwillingness to loosen its control on the economy. Authoritarian regimes can easily control the supply side of the economy, particularly if national champions like state-owned enterprises (SOE) dominate critical sectors. It is far more expensive and difficult to control consumption and the millions of financial decisions billions of people make every day.

What happens, though, when supply outweighs demand? The overcapacity of China's SOEs was a principal domestic motivator for the BRI in the first place. The PRC did not need more housing or office space; on the contrary, it had too much. But shifting from a production-based economy to a consumer-based economy required the CCP to give up its raison d'être: control. The BRI promised an elegant middle path:

keep economic growth relatively stable by shifting production to other countries. In so doing, the CCP could reap the gains abroad while maintaining a controlled economy at home.

As it turns out, the BRI has hit numerous snags since its launch in 2013. The China-Pakistan Economic Corridor (CPEC) is the Belt and Road's crown jewel, but the highly touted Gwadar port remains inoperable and much of the transit infrastructure required to link Xinjiang to the Arabian Sea remains incomplete.[27] In Sri Lanka, the government defaulted on BRI loans and offered a ninety-nine-year concession on the Hambantota Port to Beijing.[28] Many U.S. politicians accuse the CCP of purposefully taking these risks to lay "debt traps" for low-income nations, while others argue that Beijing is simply making the best out of a bad situation.

Whatever the reason, doubts are festering not only about the BRI's ability to solve China's internal economic problems but also about the initiative's solvency. According to a bombshell report from researchers at William and Mary University in 2021, forty-two countries had debt exposure to China that surpassed 10 percent of GDP and clocked in at around $385 billion.[29] The same report also found that BRI projects were on average riskier, less efficient, and more prone to corruption than China's non-BRI ventures. In 2022, the New York–based Rhodium Group found that the number of Chinese loans that required negotiation tripled in a matter of years.[30] The coronavirus pandemic supercharged these problems. BRI funding dropped nearly by half in 2020 as COVID-19 shut down construction and inhibited new projects, and 2021 was hardly better.[31]

This decidedly mixed track record has soured global public opinion about the Belt and Road. The Trump and Biden administrations have criticized the project's lack of transparency and the CCP's unwillingness to negotiate debt repayment with its partners, and the European Union is increasingly vocal about providing alternative financing to low-income countries. In 2023, Italy announced its intent to leave the project after being the first G7 nation to join in 2019.[32] That same year, the Philippines canceled a slew of projects that called the nation's continued participation in the BRI into question.[33] Xi Jinping attempted to get ahead of these concerns in 2019, when he promised a "debt-sustainability framework," vowing to cut down on corruption, boost transparency, and prioritize environmentally friendly projects.[34] Two years later, China announced a new Global Development Initiative and corresponding security and cultural initiatives to woo developing countries.[35] But it's increasingly unclear whether these adjustments can make the BRI a sustainable proposition and whether this "project of the century" is the cure-all to the PRC's economic woes. For all these reasons, it is infinitely understandable why experts like Hillman deride the BRI as nothing more than a bungled imperial gambit—or, as he cleverly put it, "the emperor's new road."[36]

TOO NIMBLE TO FAIL

Even so, the mere possibility of rapid or slow-motion collapse does not guarantee either outcome. Uncertainty is the reality of foreign policy, and shrewd leaders need to play the odds. It is a bad bet to base strategy on an adversary's worst possible outcome. America's "engagement" policy with the CCP made this mistake, and now the United States is paying the price. After four decades of giving the CCP a blank check, the United States is critically vulnerable to Beijing's malign influence and, in some cases, an unwitting accomplice in the party's ambitions.

None of this is accidental. Xi Jinping is aware of all the imperial pitfalls that threaten China's rejuvenation, and he has a failsafe: the United States. In the eight years that preceded the Belt and Road, China invested roughly $58 billion in the United States. Once the BRI took off, the PRC's investment in America more than doubled.[37] At the very moment when the CCP began behaving as a global power with revisionist ambitions, it sweetened the deal for America: more money for more access. More cooperation for deeper penetration. It provided monetary incentives for Washington to double down on its "engagement" policy. The reason was simple: the smoothest path for China to weather its tenuous economic outlook depends on robust commercial relations with America. According to Ian Easton, "If we continue to fund that and support that with our American capital and technology and managerial know-how and engineering know-how, then we will lose and they will win. They will not have imperial overreach and imperial overstretch because they'll have our help, and they'll use our funding to do it."[38]

The United States is up against an adversary with a knack for turning strengths—namely, open societies and free speech—into weaknesses. This should not surprise Americans. The CCP has proven itself to be remarkably resilient and adaptable over seven decades in the face of nationwide famines, revolutions, elite struggles, mass protests, economic restructuring, and power transitions. Its current challenges, to be sure, are difficult. Beijing's economic engine is slowing. Earlier predictions that China's economy would eclipse America's are increasingly uncertain. In August 2023 *Axios* journalist Bethany Allen-Ebrahimian bluntly reported, "The period of economic and political opening that transformed China over the past 50 years is now over, a growing number of experts say." But she was quick to caution against triumphalism: "Western analysts have consistently underestimated the ability of Beijing's economic interventions—such as subsidies, state-directed investments, and other non-market incentives—to boost new industries and power innovation."[39]

Leaders in Beijing have no choice if they want to keep their lives. Mao Zedong's aphorism remains true for China today: "Political power flows from the barrel of a gun." Success for the party is not about luxury, but survival. The stakes are high for Beijing, specifically with the Belt and Road. Xi made sure of that when he wrote the BRI into China's constitution in 2017. Failure is not a political option. As a practical matter, the PRC's foreign policy is inextricably tied up with its fate. As Nadège Rolland wrote in 2019, "BRI is not just about infrastructure building or financing; it has become Beijing's main instrument for achieving its unimpeded rise. Speculating about BRI's death," she insists, "is therefore equivalent to raising doubts about the ability of CCP leaders to achieve the most important goal that they have set out for their country."[40] Rolland was similarly astute in 2017 when she speculated that the CCP "may not consider the possible lack of economic viability to be a deal breaker. $1 trillion may simply be the price China has to pay in order to achieve its ultimate strategic objectives."[41] Beijing, not the market, is the final arbiter of the BRI's future.

Not only is the party highly adaptable; the BRI is incredibly flexible. Keep in mind: the project is bigger than ports and roads. It is no accident that the Belt and Road has proliferated over the years from a land- and sea-based project to include a Digital Silk Road, a Polar Silk Road, a Space Silk Road, and a Health Silk Road. Even with China's shrinking coffers and the pandemic's construction freeze, the BRI has continued in the form of shipments of personal protective equipment (PPE) and transfers of "smart cities" technology. Gracia Watson, a researcher at the American Foreign Policy Council, picked up on these trends in March 2021:

> Throughout 2020, Chinese tech firms introduced numerous 5G-driven medical services and helped to build 5G networks both at home and abroad to connect health care workers and patients with medical experts. . . . In May of 2020, the National People's Congress approved a six-year spending plan with 5G as its foundation. Huawei, China's controversial telecom giant, has also laid a six-thousand-kilometer fiber-optic cable across the Atlantic between Brazil and Cameroon, while the spread of digital payment platforms like WeChat Pay and Alipay has helped to further internationalize the yuan.[42]

Note the presence of Xi's other BRI tenants: policy coordination (5G networks), trade (e-commerce), use of local currencies (use of the yuan), and people-to-people exchanges (health and medicine cooperation). Researchers at the International Republican Institute in Washington, DC, identified similar trends in February 2023, arguing that the BRI was pivoting away from megaprojects toward "less flashy, less expensive model of engagement . . . in fields such as trade, telecommunications, green energy, and academia."[43]

When viewed in its totality, the Belt and Road appears to have remarkable endurance, which could bode well for the CCP's foreign policy. As Bloomberg journalist Sheridan

Prasso put it, "Even if Belt and Road spending ends up being a third of what was originally forecast, China may still have gotten its money's worth."[44] Which is to say: even a partially completed BRI could still succeed in upending the balance of power throughout Eurasia and key nodes around the world. As one CCP official put it in 2016, the Belt and Road "is not a fixed route: if one project is impossible, we will take another path! In the long run, we may even have breakthroughs where we thought we never would."[45] It's not that the BRI is too big to fail; it's too nimble to fail. But even if the Belt and Road avoids physical catastrophe, can it actually deliver for Beijing politically? Herein lies the project's true weakness.

DEADLY CONTRADICTIONS

In September 2016, CCTV1, China's premier broadcasting channel, aired a six-part series on the BRI. While Beijing also posted an English-dubbed version on YouTube, the primary audience for this series was the Chinese people. The message of the series was clear: the rest of the world loves the Belt and Road, and everyone is grateful for the leadership of the CCP. To promote that message, CCTV booked dozens of foreign dignitaries, ranging from Vladimir Putin and Henry Kissinger to former French and Australian prime ministers. They all extolled the BRI's greatness and the inevitability of China's rejuvenation. After calling the BRI a "great idea" and an "ambitious initiative," former French prime minister Jean-Pierre Raffarin held up Xi Jinping's *Governance of China* and praised the CCP's desire to "develop good relations with its neighbors."[46] In the same episode, Henry Kissinger insisted that Western governments would need to integrate China's BRI into their own views of world order.[47]

Every government seeks foreign validation for its policies, but the CCP was doing more than amplifying outside support for its actions. It was persuading the Chinese people that the rest of the world endorses the party itself. It was an exercise of proving the Mandate of Heaven: the foreign "barbarians" recognize the Middle Kingdom's greatness and acknowledge Xi Jinping's indispensable leadership.

This behavior is not indicative of a secure regime. In democracies, public opinion is reflected in polling figures, and legitimacy is earned and bestowed in elections. The people give the final blessing to rule. Not so with the Middle Kingdom. "China doesn't have a domestic political system that gives the [CCP] internal legitimacy," according to Joshua Eisenman. "It needs to have external validation from parties around the world that say, 'China's political system is legitimate, and more than that, we want to copy some of it.'" In his extensive research on China's foreign policy in Africa, Eisenman finds this same urge to use outside voices to gain domestic support: "You can see this every night on China's seven o'clock news. It begins with a parade of foreigners usually, meeting China's leaders, showing them deference, and saying, 'The [CCP] is doing a great job.' And I would say one of the primary requests—if Africans might look for some kind of external support, the Chinese side would say, 'Hey, you know, we're doing a story. Would you mind doing an interview with Xinhua?'"[48]

In this scenario, Beijing is not asking for economic favors from its junior BRI partners. It is seeking political validation to service the CCP's a priori objective: regime survival. Such behavior is undoubtedly emblematic of single-party dictatorships, but the CCP is hardly the first political organization in the Middle Kingdom to behave in such a way. From its creation and establishment, China has always sought domestic legitimacy from foreign validation. It is impossible to understand the tribute system, an expensive and economically inefficient method of commerce, apart from this political dimension. If the Chinese emperor claimed the title son of heaven, he needed a way to demonstrate to his people that it was in some way true. The optics of the tribute system—massive delegations of foreign officials streaming to the Chinese capital to perform the kowtow and receive political favors and extravagant financial gifts—proved that *zhongguo* and *tianxia* were in alignment. The domestic propaganda surrounding the BRI is Xi's attempt to make that case to the Chinese people today, at a price tag of $1 trillion. Perhaps the cost is worth regime survival, but it is worth noting that America's greatest adversary has a propensity to make economic policy in the service of geopolitics without first counting the cost. Not out of laziness or incompetence, but out of necessity and desperation.

Could China's urgent and long-standing quest to find legitimacy abroad predispose the Middle Kingdom to overextension? On paper, the possibility may appear remote. At the time of this writing, the PLA has one official foreign military base in Djibouti, while the United States has hundreds of bases across dozens of countries and territories. Recall, though, the military partnerships covered in chapter 3 that followed in the wake of BRI construction and investment. From the Solomon Islands and Kiribati to Equatorial Guinea and Argentina, Beijing seems to view the Belt and Road as a blueprint for establishing a global military presence (see map 2). The PLA admits as much in its military textbooks. Consider this excerpt from a 2018 handbook published by China's National Defense University in 2018:

Our military is "going out" into the world and integrating into the global economy systematically. . . . The military follows in the footsteps of civilian entities as they spread. The military then provides protection for civilian entities wherever they go. As the pace of "One Belt, One Road" construction and our military's march outward quicken, the trend is for our internal military-civil fusion strategy to extend out beyond our borders. . . . When expanding outward, we must use a range of tactics, pushing straight ahead and around the flanks. [We will] concurrently use methods direct and indirect, hard and soft, to realize a comprehensive security umbrella over "One Belt, One Road" countries.[49]

The handbook, *Realizing the Deep Development of Military-Civil Fusion in Our Overall Setup*, is part of a series about Xi Jinping thought. It is also the clearest articulation to date of how the CCP views the fusion of BRI civilian projects with PLA military expansion. It is an old story in international politics: as foreign economic interests accumulate, military power grows proportionally to protect those interests. For China, though, its investments in military strength are driven by more than material considerations. China is chasing more than hegemony. Beijing is grasping for legitimacy around the world at gunpoint, and inefficiently at that. According to the book, the PLA is "pushing straight ahead and around the flanks" and using "methods direct and indirect, hard and soft" to protect the party's interests. China is rejecting a choice between symmetric and asymmetric competition and opting for both—in effect, a kitchen sink strategy. This all-encompassing practice of strategy is beset with an overriding weakness: if everything

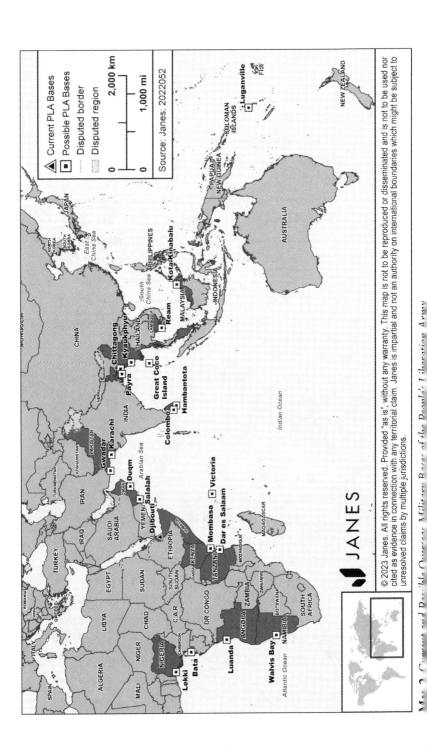

Map 2. Current and Possible Overseas Military Bases of the People's Liberation Army

Source: Janes: 2022052

is a priority, then nothing is. As China's economic growth continues to slow, this reality will grow proportionately and provide the United States with ample exploitation opportunities. Indeed, it already has.

CORRUPTION

In *Casino Royale*, author Ian Fleming paints James Bond as indifferent toward gambling: "Bond didn't defend the practice. He merely maintained that the more effort and ingenuity you put into gambling, the more you took out."[50] Although casinos are banned within the PRC (with the notable exception of Macau), the CCP shares Bond's philosophy and has instrumentalized illicit activity in increasingly creative ways. Typically, rogue regimes and terrorist groups use gambling to launder dirty money. The CCP has taken it a step further and has leveraged land leases for casinos to block the U.S. Department of Defense's expansion of its own capabilities in the Pacific. Beijing has displayed this Bond-like cunning in the Republic of Palau, an archipelago nation located a thousand miles east of the Philippines.

For decades, Palau has complicated the CCP's ambitions to project power into the Pacific. Along with the Federated States of Micronesia and the Marshall Islands, Palau freely associates with the United States. This means, among other things, that Washington determines the defense policies of these Pacific Island nations, which enables the U.S. military to permanently establish surveillance and tracking capabilities near East Asia and the South China Sea.[51] Palau serves as a highway for America and a speed bump for Beijing.

In 2017, as U.S. concerns about the PRC's expansion and aggression in the South China Sea were rising, Washington

approached Palau with a proposal to establish a Tactical
Multi-Mission Over the Horizon Radar (TACMOR) at two
sites.[52] Parking a TACMOR so close to the South China Sea
would increase America's capacity to respond to early warning
signals of PRC aggression against Hanoi, Manila, Kuala Lum-
pur, or Jakarta. This development presented clear problems
for Beijing, not just in the South China Sea but also in the
Southern Pacific where it was courting the Solomon Islands
and Kiribati.[53]

Shortly thereafter, the CCP came knocking on Palau's door,
but the emissary was not a diplomat or a general. It was Wan
Kuok Koi, also known as "Broken Tooth," a high-profile chief
of the criminal underworld. The State Department describes
Wan as "a leader of the 14K Triad, which engages in drug trafficking, illegal gambling, racketeering, human trafficking, and a
range of other criminal activities." More importantly, the U.S.
government pegged Wan as a member of the CCP's Chinese
People's Political Consultative Conference (CPPCC), a central
body in the party's global "united front" propaganda work.[54] In
other words, this Broken Tooth gangster leveraged his political
sway in Beijing not only for his criminal activities but also to
advance the party's foreign policy. How did he do this? By asking for a ninety-nine-year lease for a casino on the exact same
plot of land slated for the TACMOR radar.[55]

This detail about Beijing's effort to displace U.S. military
capabilities in Palau reveals the party's cunning and creativity.
Notably, Wan promised his Palauan hosts that the casino was
a certified and approved BRI project, a common tactic of overseas Chinese actors to conceal their illegal activity.[56] The fig leaf
concealed Wan's biggest weakness. His company in Palau, the
Palau China Hung-Mun Cultural Association, was a front in a

larger criminal network: Dongmei Group in Hong Kong, and World Hongmen History and Culture Association in Cambodia—not to mention the Dongmei Group's investments in Burma.[57] Blunting his overtures in Palau was easy enough for Washington, and it provided the perfect opportunity to hit Wan's entire criminal network. In December 2020, the Treasury Department did just that. It announced sanctions against Wan's Southeast Asian empire and blacklisted its branches in Palau, Hong Kong, and Cambodia. It didn't take long for ripples to cascade into a wave. Mere months later, Malaysian authorities conducted more than seventy raids of homegrown criminal networks with links to Broken Tooth, busted the crime syndicates, and arrested sixty-eight individuals.[58] At the time of this writing, the Air Force is moving forward with the TACMOR radar project in Palau.[59]

The episode was a success, one that the United States should replicate at a broader level. Targeting BRI-affiliated criminal networks is good, but the entities most deserving of Washington's punishment are the licit corporations directly engaged in Beijing's BRI. Just like Broken Tooth's crime empire, Chinese state-owned enterprises (SOEs) routinely engage in corrupt practices to win foreign contracts, in the form of either bribes or kickbacks. According to a 2021 report from Arachnys, a London-based consulting group, "a reported 60–80% of Chinese firms [paid] bribes to speed up projects, especially in Africa and South Asia."[60] The United States should view the CCP's corrupt practices as an opportunity to target Xi's national champions and cripple the BRI's hands and feet.

Washington could do worse than starting with China Communications Construction Company (CCCC), one of the world's largest companies and a premier BRI entity. It has more than sixty subsidiaries, employs 118,000 people, and receives roughly $70 billion in revenue each year. It has also, in the words of the *Irrawady*, a Burmese newspaper, "left a trail of controversy in the Philippines, Sri Lanka, Malaysia, Bangladesh, Thailand, Canada, Australia and Kenya."[61] In 2020, then–secretary of state Mike Pompeo singled out CCCC for its tainted reputation: "CCCC and its subsidiaries have engaged in corruption, predatory financing, environmental destruction, and other abuses across the world. The PRC must not be allowed," he warned, "to use CCCC and other state-owned enterprises as weapons to impose an expansionist agenda."[62] At the time, the Trump administration sanctioned a small handful of CCCC subsidiaries, but the U.S. government has not touched the BRI champion since. Washington has also refrained from singling out Chinese SOEs for branches-to-roots sanctions that mirror the Broken Tooth bust-up.

True, going after crime rings is easier than taking down corrupt global conglomerates. But Pompeo is right: Beijing's SOEs are Xi's primary agents in expanding the CCP's power, influence, and presence around the world. As such, the situation demands a global response. For any American sanctions on CCCC or other SOEs to be meaningful, governments from London and Berlin to Canberra and Tokyo would need to join the effort to make BRI-linked Chinese companies a pariah—a not impossible scenario, given Japan's rearmament, Australia's military cooperation with America, and Europe's increasing distrust of Beijing in the wake of COVID-19 and Russia's war in Ukraine.

No one disputes the need for a multilateral response. The question is how to secure the buy-in of our partners—many of whom have proven hesitant to stand up to the CCP. America cannot sit and wait for cooperation to materialize. There are some things only the United States can do. As revealed in the case of Malaysia and the Broken Tooth crime ring, American strength often creates room for our allies and partners to stand up and assert their own interests. Elected leaders in Washington must lead and create room for our friends and allies to join us in containing CCP expansion.

PUBLIC DIPLOMACY

Arresting the global activity of corrupt Chinese enterprises, important as it is, punishes past behavior. For America to gain a decisive advantage against the CCP, Washington must anticipate where Beijing plans to move next and head it off at the pass. To borrow the strategy of ice hockey legend Wayne Gretzky, we need to skate to where the puck will be, not where it is right now. Thankfully, the party has telegraphed its next moves.

In 2021, the Department of Defense's annual report on China's military power identified thirteen possible candidates for PLA bases: Cambodia, Burma, Thailand, Singapore, Indonesia, Pakistan, Sri Lanka, the United Arab Emirates, Kenya, Seychelles, Tanzania, Angola, and Tajikistan. The report also flagged lines of communication to the Strait of Hormuz, Africa, and the Pacific Islands as "known focus areas." The Pentagon also issued this warning: "A global PLA military logistics network and PLA military facilities could both interfere with U.S. military operations and support offensive operations against the United States as the PRC's global military objectives evolve."[63]

Before decision-makers can act, they need reliable threat assessments. Threat assessments, at their core, are estimates of an enemy's capabilities and conjectures of their intent. By that simple measure, the United States was well equipped to understand where Beijing could move next, and why it was important to stymie its plans. Unfortunately, that is not what happened. America was surprised three times over the course of eighteen months, as news broke of planned PLA bases in the United Arab Emirates, Equatorial Guinea, and the Solomon Islands—key locations in all three of the "known focus areas" the Pentagon identified. The Biden administration managed to dissuade Abu Dhabi from inking the deal, but the PLA secured port access for its naval vessels in Honiara and appears to be making progress with Malabo.[64]

The administration's response to the Solomon Islands was especially telling. When news broke in March 2022 that the PRC and the Solomon Islands had finalized the agreement, senior Biden administration officials rushed to Honiara to convince its leaders to scrap the deal. Daniel Kritenbrink, assistant secretary of state for East Asian and Pacific affairs, walked a thin line between gentle pressure and veiled warnings: "If steps were taken [by China] to establish a de facto permanent military presence . . . then we would have significant concerns and we would very naturally respond to those concerns."[65] When journalists asked whether such responses could include military action, Kritenbrink refused to rule it out.[66] Before dismissing that possibility as unlikely, keep in mind that, earlier in 2022, then–Australian prime minister Scott Morrison called the prospect of a People's Liberation Army military base in the Solomon Islands a "red line."[67]

The issue with the administration's response wasn't its concern with the deal but its lack of foresight in preventing it. Rumors had been swirling since mid-2021 that a

Beijing-Honiara agreement could be in the works.[68] Washington's haphazard response revealed America's predisposition to take small countries like the Solomon Islands for granted. The same is true of the Seychelles, one of the thirteen DOD-identified nations on Xi's wish list. Situated a thousand miles west of Diego Garcia, the location of a secretive and highly strategic U.S. military base, a PLA presence in the Seychelles would provide Beijing with a central location in the heart of the Indian Ocean. The United States, however, has no physical diplomatic presence. The State Department describes its embassy in Victoria, the Seychelles' capital, as "virtual."[69] Up until recently, America had little strategic motive to overcome the inconvenience of on-the-ground diplomacy in a remote island nation. That motive now exists with great urgency, but Washington appears, once again, slow to engage.

If the United States manages to shift gears from defense to offense, we will discover a multitude of options to complicate the PLA's expansion abroad. The BRI often spells trouble for local populations in partner countries, who are at times subject to land seizures and often edged out of employment by Chinese workers.[70] Nor does the BRI spare the environment. According to the World Wildlife Fund, BRI corridors run right through regions with 265 threatened species and intersect with Key Biodiversity Areas.[71] It should come as no surprise that the regime that wreaked havoc in the South China Sea's coral reefs and sea life is also upending the ecosystems of its neighbors.[72] Perhaps of greatest significance, governments who open their doors to the PLA have, on the whole, failed to reap material rewards. Djibouti, the site of China's first overseas military base, is also home to a PRC-funded port at Doraleh. What should have translated into a commercial boon for the Djiboutian people has somehow morphed into a cash cow for Beijing. According to Thierry Pairault, a scholar at France's National Center of Scientific Research, "Chinese money has had very limited impact for Djiboutians," and the port has been "mainly outward-looking."[73]

The game, then, is not guns and bullets but narratives and stories. In the words of Craig Singleton, a China expert at the Foundation for Defense of Democracies, "I think too often we forget about the importance of shaping and influence operations. It's a muscle memory from the Cold War that we have really lost."[74] At its prime, the United States competed masterfully in the information domain against the Soviet Union, particularly during the 1980s. By virtue of our democratic system and open society, America had a distinct advantage over Moscow: telling the truth made our regime stronger, not weaker. Hence, a great deal of America's influence operations during the Cold War were simply telling the truth about the Soviet Union's attempts to undermine free societies. The State Department did this to great effect in October 1981 in *Special Report No. 88*, which called out the Kremlin's "Active Measures" of disinformation, manipulation, and blackmail from Panama and El Salvador to France and the Netherlands.[75] The report caused such a stir that Mikhail Gorbachev complained to then–U.S. secretary of state George Shultz and pressed the Reagan administration to back away from its information offensive.[76]

To be sure, the media environment is far more complicated today than it was forty years ago. Social media platforms and encrypted messaging apps serve as highways for propaganda and disinformation and often strangle the truth before it can raise its voice. To make it a fair fight, the United States needs to take the basic step of funding information operations and breathing renewed life into this priority. Berman underscored this necessity in my conversation with him:

> Washington is more than happy 99 percent of the time to spend as much money as possible to throw good money after bad. I would say that the public diplomacy sphere is a little bit of an exception to that rule . . . in real dollar terms, the U.S. public diplomacy apparatus has effectively remained flat for something like two decades . . . the end result is that you have a public diplomacy apparatus in Washington that's fairly lackluster, and it's underresourced by any objective measure, especially when compared to the money that Beijing is spending.[77]

Realistically, funding information operations only begins to scratch the surface of America's challenges in the information domain. In the past twelve years, the post of under secretary of state for public diplomacy, America's chief messenger, has remained vacant roughly half the time. Officials at the Voice of America, the principal public diplomacy arm of the United States, are privately exasperated by the lack of willingness from both Republican and Democratic administrations to engage VOA and take the time to explain U.S. policy to foreign audiences.[78]

Much work remains to be done. Whereas the infrastructure for exploiting BRI corruption already exists, the framework to counter Beijing's exploitation is decrepit. Here, congressional attention would go a long way toward revamping America's offensive advantages in the information domain. If we enter the fight, we will find a plethora of options awaiting our use to turn prospective and current PLA bases into money pits.

PYRRHIC IMPERIALISM

The BRI has always been a means to displace the United States as global hegemon. For that to happen, the BRI must be resilient enough to withstand countervailing pressure. This question is the Achilles' heel of the entire project, for the Belt and Road is riddled with weaknesses that will not disappear even if it succeeds in building trade corridors and, eventually, military bases. These vulnerabilities are intrinsic to Beijing's political situation and unique to China's strategic culture.

As the current arbiter of China's foreign policy, the CCP is grappling with these long-standing weaknesses that prior dynasties have wrestled with and often failed to mitigate. From economic exploitation to military overstretch, the BRI's success depends on China doubling down on potentially self-defeating behavior in order to retain the Mandate of Heaven. Even if it avoids the "middle power trap," Beijing could find itself stuck with a pyrrhic victory—but only if the United States shakes off its lethargy and orients itself toward victory. No half measures will do. Winning will require America to leverage its economic policy and public diplomacy to expose the CCP's intrinsic relationship with corruption and deceit.

Recall, though, the lesson of the Broken Tooth episode. Decisive advantage comes from hitting an entire network—not just the branches, but the roots. Taking on the BRI is first and foremost a global challenge, but it ultimately leads to the initiative's roots—inside China. Prevailing against the CCP and frustrating Xi's foreign policy will require the United States to follow the BRI back to its roots within the PRC.

CHAPTER 6

TESTING RED LINES

WHEN ATTENDEES ARRIVED at the 2010 Nobel Peace Prize Award Ceremony in Oslo, there was a conspicuously empty chair. The recipient, Liu Xiaobo, was languishing in a prison in northeast China. When the student protests of Tiananmen Square swelled in the summer of 1989, Liu left the comfort of his perch at Columbia University to join the effort and even led a hunger strike outside the Forbidden City in Beijing. After serving three years of a "reeducation through labor" sentence, Liu could have chosen an easy life. He decided instead to help draft "Charter 08," a manifesto for democratic reforms in China. While other signatories were merely pressured into withdrawing their signatures, Liu's prior advocacy attracted a brutal response from the CCP in the form of an eleven-year prison sentence.

This was not a first for the Norwegian Nobel Committee. It had awarded the Peace Prize to imprisoned activists numerous times. In most cases, the oppressive regimes in question allowed family members or a representative to travel and receive the award in the honoree's stead. In 2010, however, the CCP joined the ranks of Nazi Germany as the second regime to prohibit any representation on a recipient's behalf.[1] "This fact alone," declared then–Norwegian Nobel Committee chair Thorbjørn Jagland, "shows that the award was necessary and appropriate."[2] Applause immediately swept through the grand hall and culminated in a standing ovation in honor of the absent Liu.

Like Hitler in 1935, CCP officials were furious when Liu received this distinction. Then–foreign ministry spokesperson Ma Zhaoxu blasted the award as "blasphemous," and Beijing summoned the Norwegian ambassador to register "China's disagreement and protest."[3] Liu Xiaobo's wife Liu Xia was exuberant: "I'm so excited, I'm so excited, I don't know what to say. . . . I strongly ask that the Chinese government release Liu Xiaobo."[4] Shang Baojun, one of the laureate's lawyers, was even more optimistic: "I hope on this occasion, China will open up even more, that restrictions on freedom of expression will be lifted."[5]

Instead, the CCP froze cultural exchanges with Norway, curtailed diplomatic meetings, and imposed an unofficial embargo on key Norwegian exports. PRC officials insisted that only Oslo could repair the damage caused by the Nobel Committee's independent decision. As one Chinese official put it in 2013, "Whoever tied the ring around the tiger's neck must untie it."[6] In reality, doing so would require the involvement of a stronger power big enough to stand up to Beijing.

Aside from perfunctory remarks asking China to release Liu "as soon as possible," then–U.S. president Barack Obama's engagement was limited.[7] One year after Liu received the Peace Prize, Obama insisted that "China has a different political system than we do. China is at a different stage of development than we are. We come from very different cultures with very different histories."[8] Obama, a Nobel laureate himself, was telling the same story that Biden told in 2000: China is different from America, but it is changing because America is engaging with it. Meanwhile, Liu Xiaobo languished in prison under the jackboot of a Communist Party hell-bent on resisting change.

"CULTURAL ILLNESS"

What does a Chinese political prisoner have to do with the BRI? More broadly, do human rights really matter in the broad contours of U.S.-China relations? The authors of "Charter 08" answer these questions in their opening paragraphs: "The Chinese government's approach to 'modernization' has proven disastrous. It has stripped people of their rights, destroyed their dignity, and corrupted normal human intercourse. So we ask: Where is China headed in the twenty-first century? Will it continue with 'modernization' under authoritarian rule, or will it embrace universal human values, join the mainstream of civilized nations, and build a democratic system?"[9]

Liu asked the same question Joe Biden posed on the Senate floor in 2000: When, and how, will China enter modernity? But "Charter 08" went beyond anything Biden, Trump, or any American leader has ever said about Beijing. Liu, and all his cosigners, questioned not just the CCP, but China's strategic culture:

> With the revolution of 1911 . . . [China's] authoritarian imperial system that had lasted for centuries was finally supposed to have been laid to rest. But social conflict inside our country and external pressures were to prevent

it; China fell into a patchwork of warlord fiefdoms and the new republic became a fleeting dream. The failure of both "self-strengthening" and political renovation caused many of our forebears to reflect deeply on whether a "cultural illness" was afflicting our country . . . the era of emperors and overlords is on the way out. The time is arriving everywhere for citizens to be masters of states.[10]

Unlike Biden, Trump, and the vast majority of American leaders, Liu did not ignore the crux of China's weakness: its millennia-long addiction to authoritarianism and empire (of which the BRI is a modern manifestation). Imperial Confucianism, the Middle Kingdom's habit of using territorial expansion abroad to justify its political authority at home, was hamstringing China's ability to not only modernize but stabilize. Achieving true political stability, however, would require the CCP to give up its most precious asset: control. This was the explicit demand of "Charter 08," which called for rule of law, separation of powers, an independent judiciary, democratic elections, freedom of speech, and private property—all untenable reforms for the CCP. Only one vision could survive: Liu's democracy or the party's dictatorship.

LOST LEVERAGE

Whenever people ask about my time on Capitol Hill, my answer is always the same: you never forget the legislation you drafted that passed into law, and you never forget the political prisoners you fought to free—especially the ones who ultimately died in captivity. Like Liu Xiaobo. It is a strange feeling to mourn the loss of a human you never met, much less spoke with, but the day he died was my worst day as a Senate staffer.

When I accompanied Senator Cruz to Liu's memorial service at the Washington National Cathedral in late 2017, we drafted a social media post together moments before the service began: "This man belongs to history, but he lights China's future—what it could and should be."[11]

That statement, of course, was not seen in China, as the CCP blocks access to Twitter (recently renamed X). But censors also removed posts about Liu on WeChat, while Beijing's Big Tech firms like Baidu, Sina, and Tencent "harmonized" discussion about Liu across China's Internet. On Sina Weibo, a popular search engine in China, party officials widened their censorship net to include not only his full name but his common given name "Xiaobo" in English, Traditional Chinese, and Simplified Chinese.[12] Xi's gambit was the same gamble all authoritarians make: eventually, their own people—and the rest of the world—will get distracted, forget, and move on.

At one level, the party's command of information within China is eerily impressive. They have succeeded in doing what Bill Clinton scoffed at in 2000: controlling the Internet, or "nailing Jello to the wall."[13] But their need to censor is one of their greatest weaknesses, and it stems from their fear of the people they govern. If America is to prevail against the CCP, we must never get distracted, forget, or move on. To do so would leave our adversary's vulnerability unexploited. Sadly, we have done just that for decades.

★★★★★

When Obama asked Beijing to free Liu Xiaobo "as soon as possible," he may as well have said "at your earliest convenience." And thus has it been in recent memory. Over the past three decades, human rights were the red-headed ugly stepsister of America's China policy. Washington prized cooperation with Beijing above all else. Nearly everyone was in on it. Wall Street investors craved access to China's market, and Main Street reaped the rewards, as cheaper production costs in China meant cheaper prices at Walmart and eventually on Amazon. In fairness to Obama, though, America's deal with the devil was a bipartisan affair. As we saw previously, George H. W. Bush sought to rehabilitate relations with China almost immediately after the Tiananmen Square massacre. In 2002, George W. Bush's administration parroted Beijing's talking points about its "counterterrorism" policies in its Xinjiang region, despite specious evidence of actual terrorist activity there.[14] In 2019, Donald Trump threatened to veto legislation sanctioning the CCP for its draconian crackdown in Hong Kong.[15] Whether trade and terrorism or arms control and climate, other issues consistently trumped human rights.

Over time, many U.S. policymakers siloed human rights into a boutique concern. It was all well and good for advocates to canvas Capitol Hill and sound the alarm about Beijing's stifling of religious liberty in Tibet, or the CCP's brutal organ harvesting of Falun Gong practitioners. But surely—the thinking went—these democracy activists understood that confronting China would only make these issues worse? Remember the fundamental premise of naive triumphalism: America no longer needed to make trade-offs between principles and economics. We believed we could trade our adversaries into becoming democrats.

This self-delusion was on full display in 1999, when Congress debated Bill Clinton's proposal to establish permanent normal trade relations (PNTR) with the PRC.

Then-congressman Pat Toomey boldly claimed that China was "on a voyage in the direction towards freedom":

> In China today, local villages are having democratic elections for municipal leaders. Millions of Chinese are practicing religions, including Christian religions. Workers can choose where they work for. Travel is open, including travel abroad, and almost half of economic output in China is now privately owned. Millions of Chinese citizens have access to the Internet, and there they have unlimited information and ideas, including ideas about personal freedom, political freedom, the rule of law, all of the values that we cherish.[16]

Across the Hill, Democrats were making similar arguments in the Senate. As former Senator Dianne Feinstein put it at the time, "We can work for change in China, as the benefits of trade and rising living standards bring about the goals we seek, or we can deal antagonistically with China and lose our leverage in guiding China along paths of positive economic and social development."[17] The United States lost its greatest source of leverage over Beijing by following the advice of Feinstein, Toomey, and many others. Over the past decade, however, there have been fleeting instances of Washington slowly recovering this leverage. I saw it for myself.

REDISCOVERED LEVERAGE

Congressional staff get strange meeting requests all the time. Capitol Hill, after all, is America's watering hole—a little bit of the entire country is represented in one way or another. As a foreign policy staffer, my meetings also regularly included sit-downs with foreign businessmen, diplomats, and the occasional conspiracy theorist about a one-world government. The most peculiar meeting I ever took, however, was in the fall of 2017, four months after Liu Xiaobo died, with a man named James Seng, an Internet tycoon from Singapore. His pedigree was impressive: "an Internet pioneer who developed and championed the international domain name (IDN) concept that is now the accepted international standard."[18] But Seng didn't want to talk about the Internet. He wanted to talk about Liu Xiaobo's wife, Liu Xia, who had been languishing under house arrest since 2010.

For the past three years, Senator Cruz had been pushing legislation to rename the street in front of the PRC embassy in Washington "Liu Xiaobo Plaza." The gambit mirrored an act of Congress in 1984 that designated the street in front of the Soviet embassy after famed dissident Andrei Sakharov.[19] It was one of several factors that elevated Sakharov's plight and pressured the Soviets into, ultimately, rescinding the house arrest order. Even after Liu's death, Cruz continued pushing the bill to secure Liu Xia's freedom.

The effort was about more than renaming a street. It was a competitive strategy born out of a simple net assessment: China's long-standing legitimacy problem. The CCP's fear of Liu was a microcosm of its tenuous relationship with the Chinese people. Many in Washington, however, did not see it this way. The Senate's China doves, both Republicans and Democrats, derided the gambit as fanciful, symbolic, and counterproductive. Sen. Steve Daines (R-MT) blocked the bill's progress because, according to his spokesperson, his "focus is on making change with tact and wisdom, not flashy headlines."[20] Senator Feinstein made her objections publicly. On numerous occasions the former senior senator from California stymied the bill's passage on the Senate floor, calling it a "real stumbling block" to actually helping Liu.[21]

The senators were, of course, entitled to their own opinions—but so were PRC officials. Judging by the reaction from their embassy in Washington and the UN mission in New York, Beijing was terrified. The Liu Xiaobo legislation had become a top-three diplomatic priority for the PRC's diplomacy in America, so much so that the embassy was pressuring then–secretary of state Rex Tillerson to convince Cruz to back down.[22] But Beijing didn't restrict its counteroffensive to official channels.

Mere moments after sitting down with James Seng, it became abundantly clear that I was engaging in unofficial negotiations with Chinese officials about Liu Xia. Seng was flanked by unnamed officials who quietly observed the entire meeting. Their mere presence spoke volumes and amplified Seng's message: if you want to help Liu, back off. According to Seng's telling, China's Ministry of Foreign Affairs was eager to move on from the headache Cruz's legislation had caused and was supposedly open to releasing Liu Xiaobo's wife, but China's Ministry of State Security (MSS) was blocking the decision. The subtext was clear: we needed to help Beijing save face and back off our advocacy. "This is all very interesting," I replied, "but what you're describing is a problem for Xi Jinping. Not us."

Seng and his alleged minders left the meeting with nothing resolved. It was clear to us, however, that we had touched a nerve. We had the momentum. Less than a year later, Beijing relented and allowed Liu Xia to leave China in 2018. Senior White House officials privately thanked Cruz for doing more than anyone else to secure her freedom.[23]

The parable of Liu Xiaobo and Liu Xia is a blueprint for going on offense against Beijing. Forcing the issue on human rights and making it a top legislative priority forced the PRC to respond in kind and make the concealment of its own atrocious conduct a top diplomatic priority. Every minute the PRC embassy and its UN mission spent lobbying against the Liu Xiaobo Plaza legislation was one less minute spent on elite capture and economic exploitation. It forced Beijing to play defense and respond to an American agenda they would have rather ignored. The challenge for the United States is to scale up this blueprint from political prisoner advocacy to something broader: a campaign that exploits the CCP's political instability within China—the same instability that Liu saw. Countering the CCP's grand strategy will require America to target the roots of the Belt and Road's weaknesses carefully and deliberately within the PRC. Doing so will test Beijing's red lines on its most sensitive issues and will inevitably lead the United States to two primary targets: Xinjiang, China's preeminent BRI hub; and the Great Firewall, the party's censorship mechanism and inspiration for the Digital Silk Road.

XINJIANG

Nobody is infallible, least of all the Norwegian Nobel Committee. In 1949 the panel awarded its coveted Prize for Physiology or Medicine to António Egas Moniz, a Portuguese neurologist who believed he had found a cure for depression, schizophrenia, and compulsion disorders. His cutting-edge procedure focused on the brain, specifically the neural activity in the prefrontal cortex. Moniz hypothesized that disrupting the synapses in the prefrontal cortex would liberate people from mental illnesses—an innovative possibility at the time, and the subject of horror films today. Initially, Moniz advocated for drilling holes in a patient's head that provided access to the brain, which was then pricked and prodded with a sharp instrument. Eventually, other physicians perfected a more grisly approach: an icepick through the patient's eye socket. The ordeal often left medical subjects in vegetative states, a shadow of their former selves. As one American victim of the procedure put it, "I've always felt different—wondered if something's missing from my soul."[24]

The lobotomy was a barbaric operation that bordered on medical torture. Thankfully, the international medical community has condemned Moniz's brainchild and has developed proven treatments for mental conditions that honor human dignity and actually work. Some, like the CCP, find demented inspiration in Moniz's vision and are scaling up the procedure from an individual level to a social operation. Beijing is attempting to lobotomize an entire culture and erase Uyghur identity via torture, rape, forced sterilization, family separation, and slave labor.[25] In the judgment of both the Trump and Biden administrations, these atrocities amount to genocide. Tellingly, the United States Holocaust Memorial Museum in Washington, DC, warned in late 2021 that the effect of the CCP's crackdown was making Uyghurs "slowly disappear."[26]

Ultimately, though, "genocide" is merely a word. Both America and China are parties to the Genocide Convention of 1948, which obligates all signatories to "prevent and punish" genocide.[27] Whether nations honor those commitments, or how they do so, are political decisions left to politicians. The primary challenge for leaders in Washington, then, is to channel justified opprobrium into effective strategy.

Thus far, the totality of America's response can be summed up by three characteristics: moral condemnation, targeted financial pressure, and import bans. Former secretary of state Mike Pompeo condemned the Uyghur genocide as the "stain of the century," while President Biden has challenged more leaders to condemn the party's brutality, warning that "silence is complicity."[28] Both administrations have also punished particularly egregious PRC entities for their involvement in the genocide. Penalties on the Xinjiang Production and Construction Corps (XPCC), a paramilitary organization in Xinjiang that answers to the CCP, captured a broader swath of CCP activity within Xinjiang.[29] Moreover, the Departments of State, Treasury, Commerce, and Homeland Security issued joint advisories in the Trump and Biden administrations encouraging American companies to divest their supply chains of any Xinjiang connections.[30] U.S. Customs and Border Protection has also seized various shipments originating from Xinjiang due to concerns over slave labor.[31] Most importantly, Congress passed the Uyghur Forced Labor Prevention Act in December 2021, which amounts to an effective import ban on any products from Xinjiang and other locales in China that use Uyghur forced labor.[32]

Many of these sanctions and actions are still being implemented. Some steps, if dutifully enforced, have the potential to severely hamper Xinjiang's economy. This approach is a sensible start, but it falls short in one key area: it is more confrontational than competitive. Yet again, Washington is reacting and playing defense. That's unfortunate, because the BRI, the apotheosis of the CCP's grand strategy, is inextricably linked to the Uyghur genocide. Xi is hoping and praying to whatever god he prays to—perhaps himself?—that America never discovers this glaring weakness of the BRI. Slave labor, for all its perfidy, is ancillary to the party's primary reason for cracking down in Xinjiang, namely, the territory's geographic potential.

★★★★★

Of the six BRI land routes currently envisioned and under construction, three pass through Xinjiang (see map 3). The China-Pakistan Economic Corridor, the flagship $62 billion project that provides China with land access to deepwater ports in the Indian Ocean, originates in Kashgar and runs through Tashkurgan Tajik county, on China's border with Kashmir. The New Eurasian Land Bridge originates on China's east coast but cuts across the Xinjiang Uyghur Autonomous Region (XUAR) before it passes through Kazakhstan and central Asia on its way to Europe. Finally, the China–Central Asia–West Asia Economic Corridor originates in the XUAR and cuts westward across the continent before terminating in the Balkans.[33]

True, China has alternative trade routes to Europe that bypass Xinjiang. For instance, the China-Mongolia-Russia Corridor passes through Inner Mongolia and connects China's east coast to the Baltic states. But relying exclusively on this corridor would endanger two broader geopolitical imperatives of the CCP. For one, China could only access Europe by land through Russia, which would subject the BRI's transcontinental ambitions to Western sanctions targeting Moscow's aggression in Ukraine.[34] Additionally, the BRI's logic necessitates an integration of the entire Eurasian landmass. Shifting Europe's political orientation away from Washington is indeed a principal objective of the effort—one made

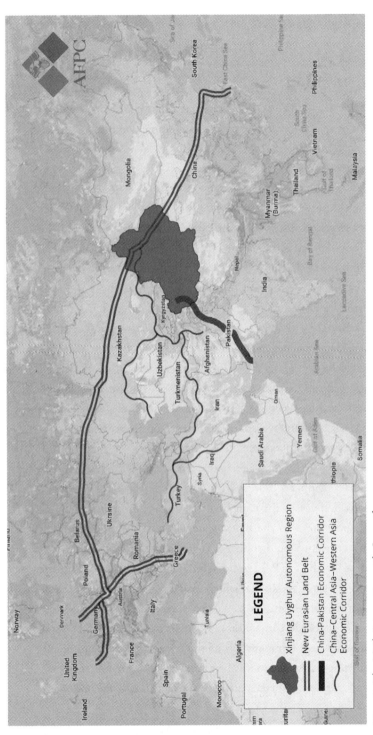

Map 3. *The BRI's Intersection with Genocide*

significantly easier if the Middle East, west Asia, and central Asia are tilting eastward as well. As Chinese state-controlled outlet Xinhua explained in 2014, Xinjiang "connects Pakistan, Mongolia, Russia, India and four other central Asian countries with a borderline extending 5,600 km, giving it easy access to the Eurasian heartland."[35]

Xi himself has telegraphed the XUAR's centrality to his foreign policy in word and deed. When China's helmsman announced the Silk Road Economic Belt—the BRI's terrestrial component—in 2013, he did so in Kazakhstan, just across the border from Xinjiang. Nine years later, Xi was even more blunt when he referred to the XUAR as a "hub" for Eurasian commerce.[36] He made these comments while praising the party's crackdown on Uyghurs. The CCP, long fearful of separatism and terrorism, seems to view the pacification of Xinjiang as a necessary condition for integrating Eurasia on its terms. Even if the toughest of existing U.S. sanctions—the effective import ban on all products produced with Uyghur slave labor—were fully and consistently enforced, the existing transportation infrastructure in Xinjiang would remain in place, commerce would continue to cross borders, and connected BRI projects throughout the continent would continue to operate.

Indeed, the CCP is the latest of several Chinese dynasties that have spilled considerable blood for control of Xinjiang. From the Han dynasty's Tarim Basin campaigns in 64 BC and AD 78 to the Tang dynasty's use of force to protect Silk Road access in AD 647, Xinjiang has long been of strategic importance to China.[37] It is the Middle Kingdom's economic gateway to Eurasia; as such, its possession is of paramount importance. The slave labor dimension is ancillary to Xinjiang's geographic potential. The CCP seems to view the pacification of Xinjiang as a necessary condition for integrating Eurasia on its terms. Geopolitics, not subsidized cotton production, is the raison d'être of the CCP's campaign in Xinjiang.

If a regime feels compelled to commit genocide for its most important foreign policy priority to function properly, something has gone deeply wrong at a practical level. The party is exposing itself to immense financial risk as it conducts high volumes of dollar-denominated trade through a region soaked in blood. Beijing certainly hopes to convert more of its trade into renminbi (RMB) to ease this financial risk, but that would not protect BRI partners in other countries that rely on the U.S. dollar.

If Washington is serious about targeting the party's strategic logic, policymakers must account for this reality. Here, a clear opportunity exists, for the United States unquestionably has the power to punish China's genocidal racket in Xinjiang. Doing so will require a unique category of sanctions, one powerful enough to strike a blow at the BRI's roots.

★★★★★

After the terrorist attacks of September 11, 2001, the United States understood that protecting the homeland required more than eliminating terrorists. America needed to target the financial networks that bankrolled groups like al-Qaeda. By their very nature, illicit networks are complex and adaptable. The trick was identifying choke points where the United States held leverage of some sort. It took barely a month for Republicans and Democrats to find it. On October 26, President George W. Bush signed the Patriot Act into law to "give intelligence and law enforcement officials important new tools to fight a present danger."[38] While the act is best known for its wiretapping and domestic surveillance provisions, it also gave the U.S. government tools to isolate and dismantle terrorist finance networks. The logic was simple: leverage the dollar's reserve currency status to force banks to close the accounts of illicit actors. As Juan Zarate, a senior Treasury Department official in the Bush administration, put it,

> We could prompt banks to make decisions to cut off banking relationships, isolating rogues from the international financial system—and we could rely on the business decision-making of the banks themselves to do the heavy lifting. The key to managing the ecosystem was to ensure that illicit and suspect financial behavior continued to be thought of as detrimental to the efficient workings of the international financial system. Rogue and criminal actors needed to be branded by their own illicit activities and isolated by those who wanted to be considered legitimate financial players. With the United States defining those parameters, we had the ability to lock rogue actors out of the system as never before.[39]

This gambit, codified in Section 311 of the Patriot Act, was a highly effective competitive strategy that Washington has used to great effect not only against terrorists but also against nation-states like North Korea. The reason is simple. America has something the rest of the world wants and needs: a universally acknowledged global currency. As such, Washington has the ability to regulate how the dollar is used—or, in the case of terrorist financing, not used.

To be sure, adversaries like China, Russia, Iran, and North Korea all are keen to demolish the dollar's dominance and clearing transactions with commodity swaps and digital currencies. Even so, the greenback's demise appears to be a possibility instead of a problem. "To date," according to the Congressional Research Service in 2022, "there is no evidence of a shift away from the U.S. dollar as the dominant reserve currency."[40]

When it comes to the Uyghur genocide, then, policymakers should consider leveraging its monetary advantage. Instead of merely blocking slave labor–produced goods from Xinjiang, Washington could sanction all commerce passing through the XUAR with the creation of a similar designation: a "jurisdiction of primary humanitarian concern." Instead of targeting individuals or entities with visa restrictions and asset freezes, this sanction would mirror existing anti–money laundering provisions by restricting American banks from providing financial services to any entity facilitating or benefiting from commercial activity within a region of gross human rights violations.

This tool, if implemented and enforced throughout Xinjiang, could effectively sever half of the BRI in Eurasia from the international dollar-denominated banking system. The underlying objective is not to punish legitimate commercial activity but rather to target trade that relies on—and exploits—persecuted and brutalized minorities. Much like laws prohibiting the importation of "blood diamonds," this authority would stymie commerce that depends on, and is inextricably connected to, similar atrocities, such as forced sterilizations, population control, and systematic repression. In so doing, the United States could leverage its superior monetary position to address the nexus between the BRI and the CCP's violations of internationally recognized human rights.

CENSORSHIP

He tried to warn his colleagues quietly. The warning signs were alarming: a strange flu-like illness spreading like wildfire through the city of Wuhan. As a physician, Li Wenliang understood China's checkered history with severe acute respiratory syndrome (SARS), particularly from Beijing's failure to arrest the spread of a SARS virus in 2003. The CCP, as it turned out, was more interested in underreporting cases and concealing infected patients in secret hospitals. Seventeen years later, the pattern was playing out again. Caught between his obligation to warn his colleagues and the personal risk of doing so, Li sent a private message over WeChat to fellow doctors on December 28, 2019, urging them to be careful. Nothing, however, is truly private in modern China. One week later, Li found himself sitting before two Public Security Bureau interrogators in the dead of night.

"In accordance with the law, we now warn and admonish you for the unlawful matter of publishing untrue discourse on the internet," the police warned. "Your behavior has severely disrupted social order . . . it is an illegal act! The public security bureau hopes that you will actively cooperate with our work, follow the advice of the police, and stop the illegal behavior. Can you do this?" Li had no choice. Standing up to the jackboots would take him away from his hospital, the very place he was needed most. "Yes," he wrote.

"If you are stubborn, refuse to repent, and continue to carry out illegal activities," the party thugs threatened, "you will be punished by the law! Do you understand?" Li signed the paperwork, affixed his fingerprints to his confession, and went on caring for his patients.[41]

Backroom threats may silence people, but they are powerless against viruses. In the CCP's coldblooded calculus, it was initially an acceptable trade-off. Soon, however, scores of people in Wuhan contracted the sickness Li warned about, posing a severe public health crisis to the CCP. Instead of responding rapidly, however, officials dithered. In January, after realizing that the Wuhan outbreak could morph into an epidemic, senior CCP officials delayed for six days. According to a damning estimate from the University of Southampton, Beijing could have reduced its number of COVID-19 cases by 95 percent if it had acted sooner.[42] Instead, during this time, local apparatchiks silenced medical professionals and ordered the destruction of viral samples. Perhaps most alarming of all, the CCP cut air travel from Wuhan to other Chinese cities but didn't bother to ban international travel— all but guaranteeing that an epidemic would metastasize into a pandemic.[43]

During this deadly delay, Li Wenliang contracted COVID-19. By this time, news of Li's initial mistreatment and intimidation had spread, infuriating scores of Chinese netizens who felt the party cared more about controlling information than stopping the virus. The blowback was so severe that the CCP had no choice but to reverse course, warning that "anyone who deliberately delays and hides the reporting of [virus] cases out of his or her own self-interest will be nailed on the pillar of shame for eternity."[44] The about-face came too late for Li, who succumbed to COVID-19 and passed away on February 6. Ironically, the Chinese people mourned his death on WeChat, the very platform that compromised Li in the first place.

Such is the nature of expression in China. Consistency is nothing; the party's interests are everything. What is a disruption of social order today could become heroism tomorrow. Indeed, the CCP posthumously bestowed the high honor of "martyr" on Li Wenliang—not to honor a public servant but to stave off public unrest. Ultimately, though, the Chinese people have little say in the matter. As one PRC expat put it, "getting on WeChat feels like 'visiting a prison.'"[45] The prison guards, Xi Jinping and his ilk, have one priority: keeping the prisoners in their cell.

★★★★★

At the time of this writing, more than one million Americans have died of COVID-19. According to the World Health Organization, the global death count is closer to 6.9 million.[46] To be sure, sovereign governments are responsible for their own responses to public health emergencies, and it is unfair to blame Xi Jinping for every single dead American. At the same time, the pandemic's origins are undeniable. What could have been contained within the PRC morphed into a global contagion. For that, the CCP bears sole responsibility.

Pundits have spilled considerable ink on assessing the motives of Xi and other cadres. Did COVID-19 originate from a wet market or from a lab? Did Beijing intentionally allow the virus to spread beyond China before it began responding? Likewise, politicians have spent the past two years blunting the PRC's global propaganda campaign. No, the U.S. Army did not bring COVID-19 to Wuhan, despite the incessant protestations of wolf warrior diplomats.[47] No, the CCP is not a net provider of public health by selling defective medical equipment to

European countries.[48] Of course, we must stand with allies like Australia who have endured economic retaliation from Beijing for daring to question China's role in the pandemic.[49]

These questions are relevant, and these responses are necessary. They are both, however, secondary. Washington is missing the pandemic's key lesson: what happens inside China doesn't stay inside China. The CCP's coronavirus cover-up is about more than the virus; it reveals the connection between the party's censorship at home and humanity's well-being abroad. Information control within China can no longer be siloed as a human rights issue; it is a national security issue. Xi Jinping cared more about controlling free expression than about stopping viral spread, and Americans died. That reality compels a focused, proportionate response from America's leaders.

Thus far, however, Washington has primarily sought to undo its fateful decision over the past thirty years to help the CCP build the Great Firewall. In the 1990s, AT&T sold telecommunications surveillance equipment to China.[50] In the 2000s, Cisco explicitly assisted the PRC in constructing Internet censorship protocols.[51] In the 2010s, American companies like Thermo Fisher worked with the CCP on DNA sequencing projects that targeted ethnic minorities within China.[52] These shameful decisions barely scratch the surface, and political leaders are understandably keen to limit further complicity. Both the Trump and Biden administrations have utilized export controls to great effect, blunting the development of China's broader tech sector by limiting its access to advanced semiconductors.

What Washington needs, though, is more than reactive measures. Hobbling the competitiveness of Huawei, Hikvision, and Dahua—China's Orwellian tech giants—could very well slash their global market share, but it is unlikely to limit their surveillance and censorship abilities within China. It is incumbent on America's leaders to move beyond knee-jerk reactions and take time to learn about our adversary. What does the CCP's response to COVID-19 say about Beijing? How are its weaknesses and vulnerabilities revealed? The bravery of people like Li Wenliang and Liu Xiaobo reveals the answer: the party's mortal fear of the Chinese people. America does not suffer from this pathology; thus, it promises a favorable advantage for Washington. It is high time to bring this second cold war onto the very terrain Beijing fears the most.

There are many who will warn that tampering with the party's censorship apparatus crosses a red line. China doves may caution that targeting the Great Firewall amounts to interfering in China's internal affairs and could invite Beijing to do the same in America. The CCP, however, is already doing this. Before the 2022 midterm elections, Meta uncovered a PRC-backed ploy to influence the outcome via Facebook accounts.[53] The CCP also has more refined methods of thought control within the United States, like TikTok, where Beijing can query search history, ping location data of 150 million Americans, and control the content they consume.[54] Less subtly, the party has repeatedly threatened economic retaliation against U.S. companies when employees dare to speak out about human rights. The National Basketball Association lost $200 million in 2019 when China nixed sponsorships and televised coverage of games. The reason? A simple post from then–Houston Rockets general manager Daryl Morey: "Fight for freedom. Stand with Hong Kong."[55]

These incidents are not disjointed episodes. They reflect a conscious decision to weaken America's political system, shape our thinking, and control our speech. The party is seeking to "harmonize" Americans—and, beyond that, the rest of the world. That is, after all, the overarching objective of Beijing's Digital Silk Road (DSR), the BRI's telecommunications component. Companies like Huawei provide more than cheap 5G infrastructure to governments looking to save a buck; they serve as the CCP's eyes and ears beyond China's borders. The surveillance capabilities Beijing is exporting complicate America's military planning, but they also corrupt Western democracies. BRI infrastructure is a means to a broader end: exporting China's political system. Which is to say: exporting oppression and instability.

It may be tempting for Americans to wish away these threats and to believe that a universal quest for freedom will ultimately doom Beijing's dystopian designs. A 2018 Stanford University study suggests otherwise. The project sought to test the efficacy of China's Great Firewall. Chinese students in Beijing were offered eighteen months of complimentary access to a Virtual Private Network (VPN), which would allow the students to circumvent CCP censors and access Internet sites outside China. The research team sent six reminders to the students over the study's duration. Only 53 percent of participants actually used the VPN software. Of that portion, only 5 percent accessed websites hosted outside China. In other words, the vast majority of Chinese students had no interest in seeking out censored information. In an effort to explain this behavior, German journalist Kai Strittmatter uncovered a surprising answer: the primary motivator isn't fear of the government. The actual reason is far more disturbing. "This is a generation," writes Strittmatter, "who with just a few more clicks could access all the information in the world. But they don't do it. They don't want to."[56]

From Chinese boy-bands singing ballads infused with communist ideology to Alibaba's "Singles Day" shopping holiday, pop culture and consumer culture have fully taken root within the contemporary Middle Kingdom. In 2019, Alibaba's "Singles Day" on November 11 eclipsed Amazon purchases on Black Friday and Cyber Monday combined.[57] The party, it seems, has erected a censorship ecosystem that has a sedative effect on those trapped inside. In the words of a Beijing-based English teacher whom Strittmatter interviewed, "[Chinese students] live in a completely different world. They've been perfectly manipulated by their education and the Party's propaganda: my students devote their lives to consumerism and ignore everything else. They ignore reality; it's been made easy for them."[58] The Stanford study backs this conclusion up: "Censorship in China is effective not only because the regime makes it difficult to access sensitive information, but also because it fosters an environment in which citizens do not demand such information in the first place."[59]

This is the world the CCP hopes to build, and it is perfecting the technology inside China. From retail companies like Alibaba to surveillance technology and telecommunications from Hikvision, Dahua, Hytera, Huawei, and ZTE, these national champions are at the tip of the party's spear to seize governing legitimacy. Even as economic growth slows, digital authoritarianism could provide the basis for a new social compact within China: stay within these high-tech parameters, and the party will provide a predictable, safe, and efficient life. "By mining insight from surveillance data," write *Wall Street Journal* reporters Josh Chin and Liza Lin, "[the CCP] believes it can predict what people want without having to give them a vote or a voice."[60]

The sheer scope of Beijing's "Brave New World" is staggering, and its success in cities like Hangzhou is well-documented.[61] Even so, the roots of the CCP's new deal with the Chinese people are rotten. Confident governments do not spend billions of dollars each year on silencing speech and blocking foreign views.[62] In the free world, information is viewed as a highly prized commodity, almost a currency unto itself. In modern China, however, information is radioactive material. If contained and channeled to state-sanctioned ends, it can achieve a great deal at low cost. If it seeps out, however, the party risks radiation poisoning and, more broadly, the unpredictable fallout of public opinion.

In 2013, senior CCP officials flagged these concerns in a notable memo colloquially titled "Document No. 9." Five months before Xi announced the BRI, his henchmen were warning party deputies against the corrupting influence of foreign ideas. The document lists seven "threats": Western constitutional democracy, concepts like democracy and human rights, civil society, the private economy, Western journalism, criticism of the CCP's history, and the questioning of CCP ideology. In its concluding paragraphs, the CCP General Office issued unambiguous marching orders: "We must not permit the dissemination of opinions that oppose the Party's theory or political line, the publication of views contrary to decisions that represent the central leadership's views, or the spread of political rumors that defame the image of the Party or the nation." Practically, this requires total control over "public opinion on the Internet" with intent to "purify the environment of public opinion on the Internet."[63]

Seen in this light, the party's considerable capability to control information begins to look less impressive. Beijing

TESTING RED LINES

exports this technology abroad under the auspices of the Digital Silk Road not to increase the free flow of information but to impede it. More specifically: to control it by censoring any and all information potentially damaging to the party's domestic legitimacy within China. Americans witnessed this long-arm authoritarianism firsthand in 2018, when a social media employee at Marriott was fired for "liking" a social media post from the Dalai Lama.[64] China exerted immense pressure on Marriott, and executives axed the worker.

As concerning as it is for an American company to be kowtowing to the demands of a foreign tyrannical government, the episode also revealed the incredible sensitivity of the CCP. It raises questions about the impact of China's search for legitimacy and the lengths to which the party may go to secure it. When I asked Matt Pottinger, former deputy national security adviser, about the Great Firewall, he likened it to "a series of bricks" that could be dismantled. "Just like the Great Wall of China," Pottinger explained, "these things can be bypassed, undermined. People can break through, and people are doing that every day."[65]

★★★★★

Unlike other conflict domains, cyber favors the offensive. Hacking is easier than fool-proofing. Whenever IT security experts talk about network resiliency, they assume that some level of penetration is inevitable. Nation-states and private actors can update coding regularly and improve malware detection, but they can never guarantee perfect protection. Cyber defense is a reactive game, one the CCP plays every day against its own people. The United States, however, appears to be disengaged and uninterested in exploiting this advantage. It is high time for America to enter that game—not merely in one-off cyber operations or espionage ploys but as an offensive actor.

To be sure, the United States has a long track record of content production and dissemination in authoritarian states. Thanks to Voice of America and Radio Free Asia, America has been publishing and reporting in Mandarin for decades. The work of the Open Technology Fund has complemented these efforts by developing tactical workarounds to the Great Firewall, primarily in the form of virtual private networks (VPNs). This approach, however, puts the onus on the Chinese people. If they are caught evading party censors and consuming foreign media, they risk their own safety and well-being.

Of course, Washington should continue its efforts to reach the people of China, but it should also open up a new front: targeting their high-tech prison. The United States should begin finding ways to make the Great Firewall more costly and less effective. In an ironic twist, America would be turning the tables on one of Beijing's preferred tactics. Beijing's "Great Cannon," a counterpart to the Great Firewall, targets foreign websites the party deems sensitive or troublesome with crippling cyberattacks.[66] The West needs a "cannon" of its own to test the vulnerabilities of China's information control. Targeting the system put the onus not on the Chinese people but on the CCP. With this approach, CCP programmers instead of innocent PRC civilians would be on the hook for censorship failures.

Selecting targets must be done with care. Inserting malware in WeChat's and Baidu's code is categorically different from hacking the PRC's Ministry of Public Security, which oversees the Great Firewall. Then again, Chinese government-backed hackers have targeted American government agencies to great effect, most notably the Office of Personnel Management (OPM) hack in 2014.[67] The following year, Xi Jinping promised Barack Obama Chinese commercial espionage would cease—a promise that China promptly broke.[68] We, too, have items of interest inside the Middle Kingdom. Unlike the party, however, our objective is not pilfering commercial secrets or personal information; the target is the system that concealed COVID-19, equips regimes around the world with high-tech straitjackets, and seeks to silence Americans. The United States is not out to steal code but to insert it. Our objective is not to hide the truth but to expose it—namely, the CCP's legitimacy problem.

Doing so would also send an unmistakable message to Beijing's BRI partners. If the United States can complicate the CCP's domestic control of information, it can do the same in any nation that relies on the DSR for modern telecommunications. Would Washington take such a campaign around the world? Certainly not. The point is to outcompete our adversary, not every authoritarian state under the sun. Making an example of Beijing, however, would serve as a warning and could undermine the political ties that underpin the DSR—which would be the final irony. The CCP is fond of making an example of dissidents—like Liu Xiaobo or Li Wenliang—to intimidate others from speaking out. As the old Chinese saying goes, "Killing the chicken to scare the monkeys." Making an example of the party's brittleness would send shockwaves through every capital that relies on Huawei, ZTE, and compromised Chinese companies: as long as America is united and strong, betting against your own people is a bad bet.

INTERFERING IN CHINA'S INTERNAL AFFAIRS

One way or another, your adversary will tell you what it fears. In 2021, Yang Jiechi performed this service in a public outburst directed at Secretary of State Antony Blinken and National Security Adviser Jake Sullivan in Anchorage, Alaska. Eleven years after berating Southeast Asian nations about "big countries" and "small countries," China's then–chief diplomat complained about America's intrepid focus on human rights: "China urges the U.S. side to fully abandon the hegemonic practice of willfully interfering in China's internal affairs. This has been a longstanding issue, and it should be changed. It is time for it to change." These remarks are a short excerpt from Yang's seventeen-minute diatribe that violated a gentlemen's agreement to speak for two minutes.[69]

The theater played well in Beijing and was viewed around the world as an aggressive instance of China's "wolf warrior diplomacy." True, China is stronger now than it was in 2010. It has not only stood up and grown wealthy; it could become a great power. But Yang's tirade betrayed the insecurity of a regime that views its own people as a threat.

Countering the BRI begins around the world, but ultimately leads back to the Middle Kingdom. Exploiting the inherent drawbacks of imperial Confucianism demands nothing less than a resolve to carefully and deliberately target the roots of China's weaknesses. By eliminating Xinjiang's role as a commercial hub and complicating the party's censorship abilities, the United States can strike a blow at the heart of the BRI and, incidentally, the essence of the CCP's foreign policy.

CONCLUSION

THE DAY BEFORE Russian president Vladimir Putin launched his "special military operation" against Ukraine, I took the train from Washington to New York. A small group of foreign policy experts, journalists, and activists were gathering at the Olive Tree Cafe, just above Manhattan's famous Comedy Cellar. On a typical Thursday night, the intimate venue hosts the world's best comedians. Our meeting upstairs was equally intimate, but this was not a typical evening. Tragedy, not comedy, filled the air as war drums grew louder. Despite dogged diplomacy, Putin had his gaze fixed on Kyiv and was poised to strike.

That night, we convened for an evening with Enes Kanter Freedom, the former NBA star who ruffled feathers in the league with his advocacy against the Chinese Communist Party. What I remember most vividly, however, were the words of Enes' host, Gary Kasparov, the famed Russian chess grandmaster, political dissident, and Putin critic. As he held forth about the policy failures that led to war in Ukraine, Kasparov condemned the naivete that deluded Washington and many

European capitals for decades. "Francis Fukuyama," Kasparov boomed, "forgot a simple lesson of history: the evil doesn't die . . . the moment we lose our vigilance, the moment we turn to be complacent, it sprouts out." Kasparov's warning stemmed from the price he has paid for standing up to tyranny: multiple arrests in Russia, physical abuse from Putin's thugs, and subsequent alienation from the country he called home. That is the choice tyranny forces dissidents to make: death at home, or alienation abroad.

Americans only understand this dilemma abstractly. To be an American is to be safe from our own government. We enjoy the dual luxuries of security and freedom. More people on Earth than we realize or appreciate can only pick one. Or, more accurately, one is chosen for them.

We are on the cusp of an era, however, when we can no longer take our good fortune for granted. The cost of being a free American is about to rise precipitously. Correspondingly, the cost of preserving a world conducive to liberty will also spike. Putin is a threat, yes, but only a secondary one. America's primary enemy in the twenty-first century is Xi Jinping and the CCP. Beijing's ambitions are global, and Xi has counted up the cost of achieving them. According to key indicators—the mobilization of reservists, wartime criminal code adjustments, increased military recruiting, and the construction of air-raid shelters—Xi is already preparing China for war.[1] That is, after all, a primary objective of the BRI: softening the political terrain to minimize blowback from Western countries if and when Xi gives the order to take Taiwan.

But the BRI stretches far beyond China's near-abroad. It is a gambit for imperial domination on Beijing's terms that stretches from Eurasia and Africa to the Americas and the

Arctic. The CCP is trying to do more than displace the United States as a hegemon. Beijing is creating a world safe for tyranny. That means, among other things, exporting their style and system of government, which in turn strengthens despots and attacks liberty. The vast majority of Americans are concerned about China and view Beijing as a threat, but few understand that the success of the party's foreign policy depends on the failure of the American-led world order and the weakening of America's political system. These are the stakes, as they were throughout much of the twentieth century: relegate tyranny to history's dustbin, or perish.

In the face of this existential choice, America's leaders in Washington are badly missing the mark. Those who still believe in naive triumphalism, like President Biden and many in his administration, are rejecting this choice as a false dilemma. They believe that evil can be neutered and tamed, civilized and modernized. Contrary to their own protestations, they are reprising America's decades-long effort to transform the CCP into a "responsible stakeholder." Such is the strength of their belief in progressivism. Simultaneously, many conservatively inclined tycoons have made a fortune in China and are now opposing any effort to counter Beijing's predations. They ignore not only the CCP's Leninist nature, but also China's imperial past. They dismiss the objective of Chinese foreign policy that spans millennia—matching its civilizational greatness with political power—because they care about their bottom line more than national security.

To be sure, many across America recognize evil sprouting back. They see the dragon for what it is—and where it is. The CCP has infiltrated our universities, businesses, communities, and government. It has shaped the fiduciary interests of

Fortune 500 companies and harnessed supply chains for critical technologies. By "following the market," many American companies have become complicit in gross human rights violations inside China. Beijing is exploiting America, as well as our allies and partners—and they are changing us.

These two problems—CCP malign influence and American culpability in atrocities—must be addressed and resolved. Doing so is an undertaking that will be measured in years, not months. American universities must value students above their own institutional interests, because CCP influence bastardizes education by teaching young Americans *what* to think about China, not *how* to think about it. Business executives should prize morality above cheap supply chains, because "never again" requires more than moralizing press releases.

This is all necessary work to blunt Beijing's predations. It is also, however, insufficient. Good housekeeping is the bare minimum, not the apex, of great power competition. We cannot "edit-undo" our way into strategic advantage. If the United States is to turn the tables on the CCP and win this new cold war, we must force Beijing to react to us. We must set the tenor and tempo of competition on favorable strategic terrain for America. Practically, this means identifying Beijing's weaknesses and exploiting them. It means performing calculated tests of the CCP's "red lines" to learn about the party's rhetoric and resolve. It means adopting a view of the CCP not as a problem to tame but a threat to mitigate. America's policymakers should aim to weaken Beijing's ability to achieve its key interests that threaten the United States and our allies. The question for us, now, is whether we will pull the lever and test our advantage. Should we do so, Americas may be surprised to find how exposed and weak the CCP actually is.

What exactly, though, does winning look like? How will Washington strategists know if their net assessments are accurate and their competitive strategies are working? Economically, Global Magnitsky sanctions on corrupt, BRI-affiliated SOEs should weaken China's commercial advantage abroad.[2] Specifically, we should expect to see Beijing winning fewer contracts in Africa, Asia, and Latin America. Eurasian trade routes that run through Xinjiang would also collapse as countries withdraw from the project altogether and de-risk their supply chains. Over time, these competitive actions could materially impact China's economy, because Xi Jinping refuses to liberalize China's market and continues to leverage SOEs for political control. America should not apologize if that happens. International politics, to quote Rep. Mike Gallagher (R-WI), is not a "polite tennis match."[3]

Informationally, successful policies would shift perceptions and media narratives within host countries and force the CCP to defend its record of exploitation. Over time, fewer heads of state from the Global South would make the pilgrimage to Beijing because doing so would imperil them politically at home. Indeed, the optics of reduced attendance at Belt and Road summits are already embarrassing for the party. Over time, these factors could suggest that the *zhongguo* does not, in fact, rule over *tianxia*. Losing the Mandate of Heaven in the eyes of the Chinese people is more than a public relations problem. It goes to the heart of the CCP's legitimacy.

That external reality, combined with America's efforts to complicate the CCP's internal censorship apparatus, should yield higher spending on internal security. Counterintuitively, that resource allocation could be a positive sign for America, provided that increased attention at home distracts Xi and the

Politburo Standing Committee from focusing on Taiwan. A more objective measure of success would be an uptick of political protests throughout China that question the quality of the party's political governance.

No doubt, some may balk at such brinksmanship as destabilizing and dangerous. Mindless hawkism, after all, is no less a betrayal of prudent statesmanship than pacifist appeasement. Let us be clear, though. It is not incumbent on representative democracies like the United States to make allowances for the CCP's pathologies. Doing so would amount to strategic codependency. As Beijing said in 2013, "Whoever tied the ring around the tiger's neck must untie it." Nor is it America's responsibility to change China politically; only the Chinese people can do that. What Washington can do, however, is frustrate Beijing's dangerous agenda. Washington need not adopt a policy of regime change across the world to do this. The failures of that approach are well documented.

We face a totalitarian regime that has adopted a foreign policy of imperialism. Imperialism is baked into China's history and sense of story. Fortunately, imperialism has a way of stretching authoritarian regimes and exposing their weak underbelly. From corruption and propaganda to censorship and genocide, the CCP has revealed itself to be brittle and susceptible to outside pressure. America can win this struggle for the twenty-first century without going to war with China.

Honesty, though, requires a full accounting. Competing to win against the CCP will come at a cost. Washington politicians will need to put country before party, because we cannot reckon with the CCP's Great Firewall if we are tearing each other apart. The American people need Republicans and Democrats to cooperate and legislate for strategic advantage, not

partisan wins. Nor can we credibly condemn Beijing's predatory foreign policy if we do not agree on what America stands
for in the world. Our allies and friends are depending on us.
They will not accept any meaningful risk with China that the
United States itself is unwilling to assume. We cannot count
on our partners to crack down on BRI corruption or corresponding atrocities if Washington remains unwilling to systematically target them.

The price, in other words, is high. It is essentially a peacetime mobilization of national power harnessed to secure an
outcome: victory, short of war. It may be tempting for some to
dismiss this framing and suppose that we can have peace without paying a price. Kasparov addressed this fantasy on the eve
of the Ukraine war. As the night concluded, he spoke of sacrifice. "That's a big word—sacrifice. That's what many Americans forgot." Hours before Russian tanks and artillery violated
Ukraine, Kasparov left us with a challenge: "I want you to consider whether you're willing to . . . make a sacrifice. Whether it's
your career, whether it's money . . . that's the story."

Looking back on that night, I hear the echoes of my 2016
meeting in Taipei, and the questions raised back then. Will we
do what it takes to preserve freedom in our lifetime? Will we
reject the fable of naive triumphalism and do the hard work of
keeping the peace? More than Taiwan is at stake. The future
of the world and the fate of American leadership are in question. Xi is using the BRI to make the world safe for the CCP.
If we are to keep the world safe for freedom, Washington must
counter this project.

NOTES

INTRODUCTION

1. James Fallows, "The Tragedy of the American Military," *Atlantic*, January/February 2015, https://www.theatlantic.com/magazine/archive/2015/01/the-tragedy-of-the-american-military/383516/.
2. Laura Silver and Christine Huang, "Key Facts about China's Declining Population," Pew Research Center, December 5, 2022, https://www.pewresearch.org/short-reads/2022/12/05/key-facts-about-chinas-declining-population/.
3. Jasmine Ng, "China Slowdown Means It May Never Overtake US Economy, Forecast Shows," *Bloomberg*, September 5, 2023, https://www.bloomberg.com/news/articles/2023-09-05/china-slowdown-means-it-may-never-overtake-us-economy-be-says#xj4y7vzkg.
4. Fareed Zakaria, "China Is Weaker Than We Thought. Will We Change Our Policies Accordingly?" *Washington Post*, October 20, 2022, https://www.washingtonpost.com/opinions/2022/10/20/china-weaker-west-policies-must-adapt/.
5. Christina Lu, "China's Belt and Road to Nowhere," *Foreign Policy*, February 13, 2023, https://foreignpolicy.com/2023/02/13/china-belt-and-road-initiative-infrastructure-development-geopolitics/.
6. Matt Pottinger, Matthew Johnson, and David Feith, "Xi Jinping in His Own Words," *Foreign Affairs*, November 30, 2022, https://www.foreignaffairs.com/china/xi-jinping-his-own-words.
7. Private conversation.
8. Richard Allen interview, Ronald Reagan Oral History Project, University of Virginia Miller Center, March 28, 2002, https://millercenter.org/the-presidency/presidential-oral-histories/richard-allen-oral-history.

CHAPTER 1. IMPERIALISM STRIKES BACK

1. Kevin Caners, "How a Mistake at a Press Conference Helped Topple the Berlin Wall," *World*, October 2, 2020, https://theworld.org/

stories/2020-10-02/how-mistake-press-conference-helped-topple-berlin-wall.

2. "Günter Schabowski's Press Conference in the GDR International Press Center 6:53–7:01 p.m.," November 9, 1989, Wilson Center Digital Archive, transcript of television broadcast by Hans-Hermann Hertle, translated for CWIHP by Howard Sargeant, https://digital archive.wilsoncenter.org/document/gunter-schabowskis-press-confer ence-gdr-international-press-center-653-701-pm.

3. "Günter Schabowski's Press Conference."

4. Albinko Hasic, "'The Gates in the Wall Stand Open Wide.' What Happened the Day the Berlin Wall Fell," *Time*, November 7, 2019, https://time.com/5720386/berlin-wall-fall/.

5. Andrew Glass, "Bush Hails Fall of Berlin Wall, Nov. 9, 1989," *Politico*, November 9, 2018, https://www.politico.com/story/2018/11/09/bush-hails-fall-of-berlin-wall-nov-9-1989-973243.

6. "National Security Strategy of the United States," White House, March 1990, p. v, https://history.defense.gov/Portals/70/Documents/nss/nss1990.pdf?ver=x5cwOOez0oak2BjhXekM-Q%3d%3d.

7. X (George F. Kennan), "The Sources of Soviet Conduct," *Foreign Affairs*, July 1947, https://www.foreignaffairs.com/russian-federation/george-kennan-sources-soviet-conduct.

8. Of course, containment as a strategy came in various iterations and variations, from Eisenhower's "New Look" and Kennedy and Johnson's "Flexible Response" to Nixonian détente and Reaganesque triumphalism. For an overview of the evolution of America's strategy throughout the Cold War, see John Lewis Gaddis, *Strategies of Containment: A Critical Appraisal of American National Security Policy during the Cold War* (New York: Oxford University Press, 1982). For a focused account of Reagan's approach to the Soviet Union, see Sven F. Kraemer, *Inside the Cold War: From Marx to Reagan* (Lanham, MD: University Press of America, 2015).

9. Adam Lusher, "At Least 10,000 People Died in Tiananmen Square Massacre, Secret British Cable from the Time Alleged," *Independent*, December 23, 2017, https://www.independent.co.uk/news/world/asia/tiananmen-square-massacre-death-toll-secret-cable-british-amb assador-1989-alan-donald-a8126461.html.

10. Lusher.

11. Steve Wright, "An Appraisal of Technologies for Political Control," European Parliament (Directorate General for Research, Directorate B, the STOA Programme), January 6, 1998, https://www.statewatch .org/media/documents/news/2005/may/steve-wright-stoa-rep.pdf.

12. George H. W. Bush, "Press Conference, June 5, 1989," USC US-China Institute, https://china.usc.edu/george-hw-bush-press-conference-june -5-1989.

13. National Security Strategy of the United States, March 1990, 12.

14. Wright, "Appraisal of Technologies for Political Control."

15. George H. W. Bush and Brent Scowcroft, *A World Transformed* (New York: Vintage Books, 1998), 89–90.

16. Francis Fukuyama, "The End of History?" *National Interest* 16 (Summer 1989): 4.

17. Fukuyama, 11–12.

18. "A National Security Strategy of Engagement and Enlargement," White House, July 1994, p. i, https://history.defense.gov/Portals/70/Docu ments/nss/nss1994.pdf?ver=YPdbuschbfpPz3tyQQxaLg%3d%3d.

19. "Bush 'Out of These Troubled Times . . . A New World Order,'" transcript, Joint Session of Congress, September 12, 1990, https://www .washingtonpost.com/archive/politics/1990/09/12/bush-out-of-these -troubled-times-a-new-world-order/b93b5cf1-e389-4e6a-84b0-85f 71bf4c946/.

20. By "Great Leap Backwards," then-senator Biden was editorializing on the PRC's "Great Leap Forward," in which tens of millions of Chinese men, women, and children died of starvation as Mao Zedong's plan to out-industrialize Western nations failed in grizzly fashion. For a full accounting of his remarks, see "TO AUTHORIZE EXTENSION OF NONDISCRIMINATORY TREATMENT TO THE PEOPLE'S REPUBLIC OF CHINA—Resumed," Congressional Record vol. 146, no. 111 (September 19, 2000), https://www.congress.gov/ congressional-record/volume-146/issue-111/senate-section/article/ S8667-7?q=%7B%22search%22%3A%5B%22H.R.4444%22%2C%2 2H.R.4444%22%5D%7D&s=4&r=42.

21. Robert B. Zoellick, "Whither China: From Membership to Responsibility?" U.S. Department of State Archive, September 21, 2005, https://2001-2009.state.gov/s/d/former/zoellick/rem/53682.htm.

22. See Joe Kline, "Daniel Patrick Moynihan Was Often Right. Joe Kline on Why It Still Matters," *New York Times*, May 15, 2021, https://www

.nytimes.com/2021/05/15/books/review/daniel-patrick-moynihan
-was-often-right-joe-klein-on-why-it-still-matters.html.

23. Glenn Kessler, "Biden's Repeated Claim He's 'Traveled 17,000 Miles
with' Xi Jinping," *Washington Post*, February 19, 2021, https://www
.washingtonpost.com/politics/2021/02/19/bidens-repeated-claim
-hes-traveled-17000-miles-with-xi-jinping/.

24. Xi Jinping is often called the president of China, a common misno-
mer. His official titles are general secretary of the Central Committee of the Communist Party of China (2012–present), chairman of
the Central Military Commission (2012–present), and chairman of
the PRC (2013–present). Because of the CCP's monopoly of political
power in China, Xi's role as general secretary is his most significant. See
Isaac Stone Fish, "Stop Calling Xi Jinping 'President,'" *Slate*, August 8,
2019, https://slate.com/news-and-politics/2019/08/xi-jinping-presi
dent-chairman-title.html.

25. Xi Jinping, "Address to the First Session of the 12th National People's
Congress," *Governance of China*, March 17, 2013, 41–42.

26. Xi explicitly unpacks his relation to Mao and Deng in his 2017 remarks
at the 19th Party Congress. See "Full Text of Xi Jinping's Report at
19th CPC National Congress," *China Daily*, November 4, 2017,
https://www.chinadaily.com.cn/china/19thcpcnationalcongress/2017
-11/04/content_34115212.htm.

27. Michael Schuman, interview with Michael Sobolik, *Great Power Podcast*, podcast audio, November 29, 2021, https://podcasts.apple.com/
us/podcast/great-power-podcast/id1593214289?i=1000543365558.

28. David Brunnstrom and Michael Martina, "Xi Denies China Turning Artificial Islands into Military Bases," Reuters, September 25,
2015, https://www.reuters.com/article/us-usa-china-pacific/xi-denies
-china-turning-artificial-islands-into-military-bases-idUSKCN0R
P1ZH20150925.

29. Gerry Shih, "Xi Offers Promises and Threats as He Calls China's
Unification with Taiwan Inevitable," *Washington Post*, January 2,
2019, https://www.washingtonpost.com/world/asia_pacific/xi-offers
-promises-and-threats-as-he-calls-chinas-unification-with-taiwan-in
evitable/2019/01/02/85ae5ece-0e82-11e9-92b8-6dd99e2d80e1_
story.html.

30. Michael R. Pompeo, "Determination of the Secretary of State on
Atrocities in Xinjiang," Department of State, January 19, 2021,

https://2017-2021.state.gov/determination-of-the-secretary-of-state
-on-atrocities-in-xinjiang/index.html.

31. "Executive Summary—China: The Risk to Corporate America," Federal Bureau of Investigation, https://www.google.com/url?sa=t&rct=
j&q=&esrc=s&source=web&cd=&ved=2ahUKEwj5_6eZt-f6A
hUmFFkFHevaAiAQFnoECA0QAQ&url=https%3A%2F%2Fwww
.fbi.gov%2Ffile-repository%2Fchina-exec-summary-risk-to-corpo
rate-america-2019.pdf&usg=AOvVaw1kdpegfqnmy3EqirOzp0Qb.

CHAPTER 2. FROM TIME IMMEMORIAL

1. For Kissinger's inclusion of Bloodworth's published work, see Robert M. Smith, "White House Inscrutable on Nixon's Cram Course," *New York Times*, February 12, 1972, https://www.nytimes.com/1972/02/12/archives/white-house-inscrutable-on-nixons-cram-course-white-house.html. For a specific reference to *The Chinese Looking Glass*, see "Dennis Bloodworth: Far East Correspondent of 'The Observer,'" *Independent*, June 21, 2005, https://www.independent.co.uk/news/obituaries/dennis-bloodworth-495967.html.

2. Dennis Bloodworth, *The Chinese Looking Glass* (New York: Farrar, Straus and Giroux, 1967), 21.

3. Henry Kissinger, *On China* (New York: Penguin, 2011), preface, chapter 1.

4. Kissinger, 10, 22

5. Dennis Bloodworth and Ching Ping Bloodworth, *The Chinese Machiavelli: 3000 Years of Chinese Statecraft* (New York: Routledge, 2017), 136–37.

6. For a detailed account of Kissinger's relationship with PRC officials and diplomats over the past five decades, see Isaac Stone Fish, *America Second: How America's Elites Are Making China Stronger* (New York: Alfred A. Knopf, 2022), 31–64.

7. Dennis Bloodworth and Ching Ping Bloodworth are quick to acknowledge this reality. See their next sentence on page 137 of *The Chinese Machiavelli*: "But their instinct when they absorbed territory was nonetheless defensive—the acquisition of more fat against the cold threat of Barbaria without—and their expansionism cultural. The emperor was not so much the conqueror of most of the states that bowed to China, as their suzerain, and he often exacted from their rulers little more than homage and tribute."

8. Alex Chan, "'The Road of Rejuvenation': A Must-See Exhibition," *China Daily*, July 19, 2018, http://www.chinadaily.com.cn/a/2018 07/19/WS5b50642ba310796df4df780b.html.

9. "Memorandum of Conversation between Chairman Mao Zedong and President Richard Nixon," Wilson Center Digital Archive, February 21, 1972, https://digitalarchive.wilsoncenter.org/document/memor andum-conversation-between-chairman-mao-zedong-and-president -richard-nixon.

10. William Safire, "The Biggest Vote," *New York Times*, May 18, 2000, https://www.nytimes.com/2000/05/18/opinion/essay-the-biggest -vote.html.

11. Tara Francis Chan, "State Department Official on China Threat: For First Time U.S. Has 'Great Power Competitor That Is Not Caucasian,'" *Newsweek*, May 2, 2019, https://www.newsweek.com/china -threat-state-department-race-caucasian-1413202.

12. Sun Tzu, *The Art of War*, trans. Lionel Giles, Chinese Text Project, https://ctext.org/art-of-war/laying-plans.

13. Sun Tzu, *Art of War*, https://ctext.org/art-of-war/attack-by-stratagem.

14. For a resource that takes the reader beyond a cliché and into the history of China's military strategy, see Ralph D. Sawyer, *The Tao of Deception: Unorthodox Warfare in Historic and Modern China* (New York: Basic Books, 2007). For primary source dynastic-era literature on military strategy, see Ralph D. Sawyer, *The Seven Military Classics of Ancient China* (New York: Basic Books, 2007).

15. The Policy Planning Staff, Office of the Secretary of State, *The Elements of the China Challenge*, U.S. Department of State, November 2020, p. 33, https://www.state.gov/wp-content/uploads/2020/11/20-02832 -Elements-of-China-Challenge-508.pdf.

16. Josh Rogin, *Chaos under Heaven: Trump, Xi, and the Battle for the 21st Century* (New York: Houghton Mifflin Harcourt, 2021), 109–14.

17. This understanding of strategic culture as the interplay of story, identity, and behavior resonates with the scholarship of Jack Snyder and Colin Gray. Under the auspices of the RAND Corporation, Snyder published a paper about Soviet strategic culture and nuclear policy in 1977 and defined strategic culture as "the sum total of ideas, conditioned emotional responses, and patterns of behavior that members of a national strategic community have acquired through instruction or imitation and share with each other with regard to nuclear

strategy." See Jack Snyder, "The Soviet Strategic Culture: Implications for Limited Nuclear Operations," RAND Corporation, September 1977, https://www.rand.org/content/dam/rand/pubs/reports/2005/R2154.pdf. Four years later, Colin Gray, a strategist at the Washington, DC–based Hudson Institute, characterized American strategic culture as "a distinctively American way in strategic matters" defined by "modes of thought and action with respect to force, deriv[ed] from perception of the national historical experience, aspiration for self-characterization . . . and from all of the many distinctively American experiences . . . that characterize an American citizen." See Colin S. Gray, "National Style in Strategy: The American Example," *International Security* 6, no. 2 (Fall 1981): 22. In the 1990s, Alastair Iain Johnston of Harvard University examined the Ming dynasty's grand strategy against its northern Mongol neighbors through the prism of strategic culture. Johnston defined strategic culture as "an integrated system of symbols (i.e., argumentation structures, languages, analogies, metaphors, etc.) that acts to establish pervasive and long-lasting grand strategic preferences by formulating concepts of the role and efficacy of military force in interstate political affairs." See Alastair Iain Johnston, *Cultural Realism: Strategic Culture and Grand Strategy in Chinese History* (Princeton: Princeton University Press, 1995), 36. For an exploration of why these different definitions matter, see Gray, "Strategic Culture as Context: The First Generation of Theory Strikes Back," *Review of International Studies* 25, no. 1 (1999): 49–69.

18. On April 14, 2011, PRC diplomats at the United Nations appealed to "abundant historical and legal evidence" for China's "indisputable sovereignty" over the South China Sea. See PRC, *China Note Verbale to the United Nations*, CML/8/2011, April 14, 2011, https://www.un.org/depts/los/clcs_new/submissions_files/mysvnm33_09/chn_2011_re_phl_e.pdf. The CCP's sovereignty claims over Taiwan go back to the inception of the PRC. In a 1958 diplomatic cable, State Department officials scoff at Beijing's claim over Taipei "from 'time immemorial,'" citing America's liberation of Taiwan from Japanese colonization in World War II. See Office of the Historian, "109. Telegram from the Department of State to the Embassy in Poland," *Foreign Relations of the United States, 1958–1960, China, Volume XIX*, https://history.state.gov/historicaldocuments/frus1958-60v19/d109. In 2004, a PRC government spokesperson asserted China's claim over the Japanese-administered

Senkaku Islands "since time immemorial." See Joseph Kahn, "China Tells Japan to Release 7 Arrested on Disputed Island," *New York Times*, March 26, 2004, https://www.nytimes.com/2004/03/26/world/chi na-tells-japan-to-release-7-arrested-on-disputed-island.html.

19. "If Treasures Could Talk: How China's Name Originated," *CGTN*, April 19, 2018, https://news.cgtn.com/news/77516a4e356b7a63335 66d54/share_p.html.

20. For a brief commentary on China's civilizational and social superiority relative to its neighbors, see Asım Doğan, *Hegemony with Chinese Characteristics: From the Tributary System to the Belt and Road Initiative* (New York: Routledge, 2021), 41–42.

21. For a brief investigation of what these raids looked like during the Shang (1600 BC–1045 BC) and Zhou (1046 BC–256 BC) eras, see Michael Schuman, *Superpower Interrupted: The Chinese History of the World* (New York: PublicAffairs, 2020), 36–37.

22. Schuman, 28.

23. Doğan, *Hegemony*, 42.

24. Howard W. French, *Everything under the Heavens: How the Past Helps Shape China's Push for Global Power* (New York: Vintage Books, 2018), 134.

25. Yan Xuetong, *Ancient Chinese Thought, Modern Chinese Power* (Princeton: Princeton University Press, 2011), 218.

26. Charles O. Hucker, *China's Imperial Past: An Introduction to Chinese History and Culture* (Stanford: Stanford University Press, 1975), 55.

27. Bloodworth, *Chinese Looking Glass*, 149.

28. June Teufel Dreyer, *Middle Kingdom and Empire of the Rising Sun: Sino-Japanese Relations, Past and Present* (Oxford: Oxford University Press, 2018), 5.

29. David Kang, *East Asia before the West: Five Centuries of Trade and Tribute* (New York: Columbia University Press, 2012), 81.

30. Bloodworth and Bloodworth, *Chinese Machiavelli*, 137.

31. China's tribute system has attracted significant debate in academia, as some scholars have questioned the significance or even the existence of the system. For an exposition of those debates and a response, see Kang, *East Asia before the West*.

32. Kenneth Scott Latourette, *The Chinese: Their History and Culture* (New York: Macmillan, 1964), 71.

33. See Lin Gan, *A General History of the Xiongnu*, trans. Duan Manfu, Lin Yang, and Song Min (Salt Lake City: American Academic Press, 2020), 54. See also René Grousset, *The Empire of the Steppes: A History of Central Asia*, translated by Naomi Walford (New Brunswick: Rutgers University Press, 1970), 26.

34. See Latourette, *The Chinese*, 71. See also Hucker, *China's Imperial Past*, 45.

35. Carrie Gracie, "Qin Shi Huang: The Ruthless Emperor Who Burned Books," BBC, October 15, 2012, https://www.bbc.com/news/magazine-19922863.

36. While Confucianism and legalism illuminate the imperial elements of China's strategic culture, they hardly constitute the totality of China's unique approach to statecraft. For an exploration of Taoism and various strands of Chinese strategic culture, see Derek M. C. Yuen, "The System of Chinese Strategic Thought," *Comparative Strategy* 29, no. 3 (2010): 245–59.

37. Bloodworth, *Chinese Looking Glass*, 42.

38. Pamala Kyle Crossley, *A Translucent Mirror: History and Identity in Qing Imperial Ideology* (Berkley: University of California Press, 1999), 227.

39. Doğan, *Hegemony*, 51.

40. Doğan, 137. As we will see in chapter 5, this search for legitimacy has served to bait China into strategic overstretch at multiple points throughout its history.

41. See Latourette, *The Chinese*, 82, and Schuman, *Superpower Interrupted*, 70–71.

42. See Schuman, 71.

43. See Schuman, 68–69.

44. See Hucker, *China's Imperial Past*, 139.

45. For conquest and colonization of modern-day Xinjiang, see Schuman, *Superpower Interrupted*, 93; and Grousset, *Empire of the Steppes*, 99–101, 103, 107–8, and 115. For protectorates in central Asia, see Grousset, 118–19.

46. See Grousset, 289–91.

47. See Geoff Wade, "The Zheng He Voyages: A Reassessment," *Journal of the Malaysian Branch of the Royal Asiatic Society* 78, no. 1 (2005): 37–58.

48. The term "genocide" is loaded with legal and moral weight and should thus be used with precision. In the case of the Qing's extermination of

the Dzunghars, evidence exists of the dynasty's intent to destroy the
Dzunghars in whole or in part via mass killings and depopulation. See
Crossley, *Translucent Mirror*, 320–21, 326–27.

49. Some scholars dispute this characterization of China's history. Timothy
Brook, for instance, argues that a decisive break occurs between the Song
dynasty and the Yuan dynasty, which marked the conquest of China by
Mongolia under the leadership of Genghis Khan and Kublai Khan.
According to Brook's argument, Mongolia's occupation of China was the
Middle Kingdom's "second great unification," as important and distinct
as the establishment of China under the Qin in 221 BC. As Brook puts
it, "What changed with the coming of the Mongols was the deeper con-
viction that [the Mandate of Heaven] entailed the right to expand the
authority of [the emperor's family] out across the entire world, incor-
porating all existing polities and rulers into a system in which military
power is paramount." Brook is right to emphasize the importance of
the Mongol conquest, but he downplays the imperial roots inherent in
China's self-identity for thousands of years. See Timothy Brook, *Great
State: China and the World* (New York: HarperCollins, 2020), 7–8.

50. Interview with Elon Musk, "Elon Musk: War, AI, Aliens, Politics,
Physics, Video Games, and Humanity," *Lex Fridman Podcast*, November 9, 2023, https://www.youtube.com/watch?v=JN3KPFbWCy8.

51. See Johnston, *Cultural Realism*, 27.

52. Quoted in Geremie R. Barmé, "Burn the Books, Bury the Scholars!,"
China File, August 22, 2017, https://www.chinafile.com/reporting
-opinion/viewpoint/burn-books-bury-scholars.

53. See Christopher A. Ford, *The Mind of Empire: China's History and
Modern Foreign Relations* (Lexington: University Press of Kentucky,
2010), 190.

54. China scholars differ on the broader question of the PRC's relationship
to China's imperial past. Did the founding of the PRC in 1949 mark a
break with China's civilizational heritage and strategic culture, or was
it a continuation of those things? A proper exposition of that debate is
beyond the scope of this book, but Christopher Ford summarizes the
contours ably. For that, and his argument that Mao's Global South policy mirrored Chinese dynastic policies, see Ford, 211–15.

55. See Deng Xiaoping, "Speech at the Third Plenary Session of the Central Advisory Commission of the Communist Party of China," October
22, 1984, https://dengxiaopingworks.wordpress.com/2013/03/18/

speech-at-the-third-plenary-session-of-the-central-advisory-commis
sion-of-the-communist-party-of-china/.

56. "President Jiang's Speech at Harvard University, 1997," USC US-China Institute, November 1, 1997, https://china.usc.edu/president-jiangs -speech-harvard-university-1997.

57. George W. Bush, *Decision Points* (New York: Crown Publishers, 2010), 427.

58. Hu Jintao's mantra of a "Harmonious Society" caught the attention of several China scholars at the time, several of whom noted the resonance with the Mandate of Heaven. See Jonathan Watts, "China's President Borrows from Confucius," *Guardian*, https://www.theguardian.com/ guardianweekly/story/0,,1742975,00.html.

59. See Chris Buckley, "Leader Taps into Chinese Classics in Seeking to Cement Power," *New York Times*, October 11, 2014, https://www.ny times.com/2014/10/12/world/leader-taps-into-chinese-classics-in -seeking-to-cement-power.html.

60. Buckley.

61. Sun Tzu, *Art of War*, https://ctext.org/art-of-war/attack-by-strata gem.

62. Well before the Chinese Communist Party came into power in 1949, thoughts of *tianxia*, the tribute system, and empire were alive and well during China's Republican era. See French, *Everything under the Heavens*, 70–73.

CHAPTER 3. MIDDLE KINGDOM RESURGENT

1. Xi Jinping, "Work Together to Build the Silk Road Economic Belt," *The Governance of China* (Beijing: Foreign Languages Press, 2014), 317.

2. Xi.

3. Bruno Maçães, *Belt and Road: A Chinese World Order* (London: Hurst, 2018), 8.

4. For a comprehensive account of the BRI's funding mechanisms, areas of focus, and execution, see Daniel Drache, A. T. Kingsmith, and Duan Qi, *One Road, Many Dreams: China's Bold Plan to Remake the Global Economy* (London: Bloomsbury China, 2019). See also Nadège Rolland, *China's Eurasian Century? Political and Strategic Implications of the Belt and Road Initiative* (New Delhi: Pentagon Press, 2018).

5. "China Voice: Confontation, Exclusiveness Betray Silk Road Spirit," Consulate General of the People's Republic of China in New York,

June 25, 2014, http://newyork.china-consulate.gov.cn/eng/xw/2014 06/t20140625_4706736.htm.

6. Xi, "Work Together to Build the Silk Road Economic Belt," 315.

7. Michael Schuman, *Superpower Interrupted: The Chinese History of the World* (New York: PublicAffairs, 2020), 65–69.

8. Xi Jinping, Speech by Chinese President Xi Jinping to Indonesian Parliament, October 3, 2013, http://www.asean-china-center.org/eng lish/2013-10/03/c_133062675.htm.

9. Schuman, *Superpower Interrupted*, 178.

10. Secretary of Defense James N. Mattis, Remarks by Secretary Mattis at the U.S. Naval War College Commencement, Newport, Rhode Island, June 15, 2018, https://www.defense.gov/News/Transcripts/Tran script/Article/1551954/remarks-by-secretary-mattis-at-the-us-naval -war-college-commencement-newport-rh/.

11. Kent E. Calder, *Super Continent: The Logic of Eurasian Integration* (Stanford: Stanford University Press, 2019), 18, 20.

12. Calder, 19.

13. Drache, Kingsmith, and Duan, *One Road, Many Dreams*, 221.

14. Drache, Kingsmith, and Duan, 219–20.

15. Drache, Kingsmith, and Duan, 222.

16. Drache, Kingsmith, and Duan, 217.

17. See Ian Easton, *The Final Struggle: Inside China's Global Grand Strategy* (Manchester: Eastbridge Books, 2022), 61.

18. For a detailed explanation of this ideological analysis, see Easton, 53–69.

19. Rolland, *China's Eurasian Century*, 135.

20. Rolland, 135.

21. Rolland, 137.

22. Dan Tobin, "How Xi Jinping's 'New Era' Should Have Ended U.S. Debate on Beijing's Ambitions," testimony before the U.S.-China Economic and Security Review Commission, March 13, 2020, https:// www.uscc.gov/sites/default/files/testimonies/SFR%20for%20US CC%20TobinD%2020200313.pdf.

23. Angela Stanzel, "China's Belt and Road—New Name, Same Doubts?" European Council on Foreign Relations, May 19, 2017, https://ecfr .eu/article/commentary_chinas_belt_and_road_new_name_same_ doubts/.

24. John Pomfret, "U.S. Takes a Tougher Tone with China," *Washington Post*, July 30, 2010, https://www.washingtonpost.com/wp-dyn/con tent/article/2010/07/29/AR2010072906416.html.

25. Derek Scissors, "China Global Investment Tracker," American Enterprise Institute, https://www.aei.org/china-global-investment-tracker/.

26. Scissors.

27. See Duncan Forgan, "New Semi-High-Speed Train Makes Laos More Accessible Than Ever," CNN, November 9, 2022, https://www.cnn .com/travel/article/china-laos-semi-high-speed-train/index.html.

28. See RFA Staff, "China Navy Facility in Cambodia Raises Eyebrows in Vietnam and Beyond," Radio Free Asia, June 8, 2022, https://www.rfa .org/english/news/cambodia/china-base-06082022100523.html.

29. "Roundup: BRI Projects Help Deepen Cambodia-China Cooperation: Cambodian Officials, Experts," Xinhua, October 29, 2022, https:// english.news.cn/20221029/b732e4c2febf4fbf906d09f6df1a8f82/c .html.

30. Asia Maritime Transparency Initiative, "China Island Tracker," Center for Strategic and International Studies, https://amti.csis.org/island -tracker/china/.

31. "China's Maritime Disputes, 1895–2020," Council on Foreign Relations, https://www.cfr.org/timeline/chinas-maritime-disputes.

32. Manuel Mogato, Michael Martina, and Ben Blanchard, "ASEAN deadlocked on South China Sea, Cambodia Blocks Statement," Reuters, July 25, 2016, https://www.reuters.com/article/us-southchinasea-rul ing-asean/asean-deadlocked-on-south-china-sea-cambodia-blocks -statement-idUSKCN1050F6.

33. Sir Halford John Mackinder, *Democratic Ideals and Reality: A Study in the Politics of Reconstruction* (New York: Henry Holt and Company, 1919), 186.

34. "In Their Own Words: Joint Statement of the Russian Federation and the People's Republic of China on the International Relations Entering a New Era and the Global Sustainable Development," China Aerospace Studies Institute, February 4, 2022, https://www.airuniversity .af.edu/Portals/10/CASI/documents/Translations/2022-02-04%20 China%20Russia%20joint%20statement%20International%20Rela tions%20Entering%20a%20New%20Era.pdf.

35. Farnaz Fassihi and Steven Lee Myers, "China, with $400 Billion Iran Deal, Could Deepen Influence in Mideast," *New York Times*, March 27,

2021, https://www.nytimes.com/2021/03/27/world/middleeast/china-iran-deal.html.

36. Scissors, "China Global Investment Tracker."

37. "China Focus: Xinjiang Becomes Logistics Hub of Belt and Road," Xinhua, August 12, 2018, http://www.xinhuanet.com/english/2018 -08/12/c_137384382.htm.

38. Hui Lu, Charlene Rohr, Marco Hafner, and Anna Knack, *China Belt and Road Initiative: Measuring the Impact of Improving Transportation Connectivity on Trade in the Region* (Santa Monica, CA: RAND Corporation, 2018), https://www.rand.org/pubs/research_reports/RR26 25.html.

39. To be sure, these pre-pandemic estimates are a thing of the past, not the present. As we will see in chapter 5, the BRI shifted significantly in the wake of COVID-19 and China's own internal economic issues. For the referenced figures, see François de Soyres, Alen Mulabdic, and Michele Ruta, "Common Transport Infrastructure: A Quantitative Model and Estimates from the Belt and Road Initiative," World Bank Group, April 2019, http://documents1.world bank.org/curated/en/879031554144957551/pdf/Common-Tran sport-Infrastructure-A-Quantitative-Model-and-Estimates-from-the -Belt-and-Road-Initiative.pdf.

40. James Kynge, "China's Blueprint for an Alternative World Order," *Financial Times*, August 23, 2023, https://www.ft.com/content/8ac 52fe7-e9db-48a8-b2f0-7305ab53f4c3.

41. United Nations Human Rights Council, A/HRC/41/G/17, "Promotion and Protection of All Human Rights, Civil, Political, Economic, Social and Cultural Rights, Including the Right to Development," August 9, 2019, https://documents-dds-ny.un.org/doc/UNDOC/ GEN/G19/240/77/PDF/G1924077.pdf?OpenElement.

42. See Michael Sobolik, "Primary Jurisdiction of Humanitarian Concern: A New Tool to Blunt China's Campaign in Xinjiang," American Foreign Policy Council, September 25, 2020, p. 5, https://www.afpc .org/uploads/documents/IPSP_Memorandum-Xinjiang_FINAL_ PAPER.pdf.

43. Loveday Morris, Emily Rauhala, and John Hudson, "German Leader Scholz Visits China's Xi amid Misgiving from His Allies," *Washington Post*, November 3, 2022, https://www.washingtonpost.com/world/ 2022/11/03/olaf-scholz-china-trip-germany/.

44. "China, Kiribati Sign MOU on Belt and Road Cooperation," Xinhua, January 6, 2020, http://www.xinhuanet.com/english/asiapacific/2020 -01/06/c_138682716.

45. Natalie Whiting, Christina Zhou, and Kai Feng, "What Does It Take for China to Take Taiwan's Pacific Allies? Apparently, $730 Million," *ABC News*, September 18, 2019, https://www.abc.net.au/news/2019 -09-18/solomon-islands-cuts-ties-with-taiwan-in-favour-of-china/ 11524118.

46. Jonathan Barrett, "China Plans to Revive Strategic Pacific Airstrip, Kiribati Lawmaker Says," Reuters, May 5, 2021, https://www.reuters .com/article/us-china-kiribati-exclusive/china-plans-to-revive-strate gic-pacific-airstrip-kiribati-lawmaker-says-idUSKBN2CM0IZ.

47. Hu Yuwei and Bai Yunyi, "Kiribati to Ink 10 MOUs with China— a True, Trusted Friend to South Pacific Countries: Ambassador," *Global Times*, May 27, 2022, https://www.globaltimes.cn/page/202 205/1266706.shtml.

48. Kirsty Needham, "EXCLUSIVE Solomon Islands Considers Security Cooperation with China—Official," Reuters, March 24, 2022, https:// www.reuters.com/world/exclusive-solomon-islands-considers-secu rity-cooperation-with-china-official-2022-03-24/.

49. Ellen Nakashima and Cate Cadell, "China Secretly Building Naval Facility in Cambodia, Western Officials Say," *Washington Post*, June 6, 2022, https://www.washingtonpost.com/national-security/2022/06/ 06/cambodia-china-navy-base-ream/.

50. See Robert C. O'Brien, "American Pacific Islanders Deserve Protec-tion—In the Pacific," *Diplomat*, June 30, 2021, https://thediplomat .com/2021/06/american-pacific-islanders-deserve-protection-in -the-pacific/.

51. See Marian Faa, "'No Slowing Down' of Military Presence in Mari-ana Islands," ABC Radio Australia, March 22, 2021, https://www.abc .net.au/radio-australia/programs/pacificbeat/us-military-in-north ern-mariana-islands-raises-concern/13266772. See also Yuan Zhi (Owen) Ou, "The Northern Mariana Islands: US Territory, China -Dependent," *Diplomat*, September 25, 2021, https://thediplomat .com/2021/09/the-northern-mariana-islands-us-territory-china-de pendent/. See chapter 5 for China's economic exploitation of Palau.

52. See Cleo Paskal, "Taiwan Does What Needs to Be Done for Daniel Suidani, and for Us All," *Sunday Guardian*, July 10, 2021, https://sun dayguardianlive.com/news/taiwan-needs-done-daniel-suidani-us.

53. Lord Curzon of Kedleston, *The Place of India in the Empire: Being an Address Delivered before the Philosophical Institute of Edinburgh* (London: John Murray, 1909), 2.

54. Curzon, 12.

55. Laura Silver, Christine Huang, and Laura Clancy, "Key Facts as India Surpasses China as the World's Most Populous Country," Pew Research Center, February 9, 2023, https://www.pewresearch.org/fact-tank/2023/02/09/key-facts-as-india-surpasses-china-as-the-worlds-most-populous-country/.

56. Anjana Pasricha, "India Skips China Belt and Road Summit amid Concerns," Voice of America, May 16, 2017, https://www.voanews.com/a/india-skips-china-belt-and-road-summit/3852687.html.

57. See Jeff Smith, "China-India Relations in the Modi-Xi Era," testimony before the US-China Economic and Security Review Commission, March 10, 2016, https://www.uscc.gov/sites/default/files/SMITH_Remarks%20031016.pdf.

58. Scissors, "China Global Investment Tracker."

59. "Nepal, China Sign Bilateral Cooperation Agreement under Belt and Road Initiative," Xinhua, May 12, 2017, http://www.xinhuanet.com/english/2017-05/12/c_136276949.htm.

60. P. K. Balachandran, "Nepal Backs Away from US State Partnership Program," *Diplomat*, June 22, 2022, https://thediplomat.com/2022/06/nepal-backs-away-from-us-state-partnership-program/.

61. Devjyot Ghoshal, Anand Katakam, and Anditi Bhandari, "China Steps Up Construction along Disputed Bhutan Border," Reuters, January 12, 2022, https://www.reuters.com/graphics/CHINA-BHUTAN/BORDER/zjvqknaryvx/.

62. Author interview with Ilan Berman, "China and the Middle East," *Great Power Podcast*, January 13, 2022, https://podcasts.apple.com/us/podcast/great-power-podcast/id1593214289?i=1000546346706.

63. Scissors, "China Global Investment Tracker."

64. Gordon Lubold and Warren P. Strobel, "Secret Chinese Port Project in Persian Gulf Rattles U.S. Relations with U.A.E.," *Wall Street Journal*, November 19, 2021, https://www.wsj.com/articles/us-china-uae-military-11637274224.

65. John Hudson, Ellen Nakashima, and Liz Sly, "Buildup Resumed at Suspected Chinese Military Site in UAE, Leak Says," *Washington Post*, April 26, 2023, https://www.washingtonpost.com/national-security/2023/04/26/chinese-military-base-uae/.

66. See Peter Baker, "Chinese-Brokered Deal Upends Mideast Diplomacy and Challenges U.S.," *New York Times*, March 11, 2023, https://www.nytimes.com/2023/03/11/us/politics/saudi-arabia-iran-china-biden.html.

67. Scissors, "China Global Investment Tracker."

68. Dickens Olewe, "Why African Countries Back China on Human Rights," BBC, May 2, 2021, https://www.bbc.com/news/world-africa-56717986.

69. Joshua Eisenman, interview with Michael Sobolik, *Great Power Podcast*, April 22, 2022, https://podcasts.apple.com/us/podcast/great-power-podcast/id1593214289?i=1000558387096.

70. For background on China's base in Djibouti, see Max Bearak, "In Strategic Djibouti, a Microcosm of China's Growing Foothold in Africa," *Washington Post*, December 30, 2019, https://www.washingtonpost.com/world/africa/in-strategic-djibouti-a-microcosm-of-chinas-growing-foothold-in-africa/2019/12/29/a6e664ea-beab-11e9-a8b0-7ed8a0d5dc5d_story.html. For a possible base in Equatorial Guinea, see Michael M. Phillips, "China Seeks First Military Base on Africa's Atlantic Coast, U.S. Intelligence Finds," *Wall Street Journal*, December 5, 2021, https://www.wsj.com/articles/china-seeks-first-military-base-on-africas-atlantic-coast-u-s-intelligence-finds-11638726327.

71. Scissors, "China Global Investment Tracker."

72. "China Urges Progress on Myanmar Belt & Road Projects, Backs Peace Efforts," Radio Free Asia, January 12, 2021, https://www.rfa.org/english/news/myanmar/wang-01122021213137.html.

73. Wan Ming, "Zheng He's Seven Voyages into the Namoli Ocean—the Indian Ocean," *China and Asia* 1 (2019): 118.

74. Mark P. Sullivan and Thomas Lum, "China's Engagement with Latin America and the Caribbean," Congressional Research Service, December 14, 2021, https://crsreports.congress.gov/product/pdf/IF/IF10982/13.

75. Megan Janetsky, "Taiwan's President Seeks to Strengthen Relations with Allies in Central America Visit," Associated Press, April 1, 2023,

https://www.pbs.org/newshour/world/taiwans-president-seeks-to
-strengthen-relations-with-allies-in-central-america-visit.

76. Sofia Menchu and Ted Hesson, "Under US pressure on Graft, El Salvador Ratifies Cooperation Deal with China," Reuters, May 18, 2021,
https://autos.yahoo.com/under-u-pressure-graft-el-160952913.html.

77. Ken Dalanian, Joel Seidman, and Gabriel Sanchez, "A Project in El
Salvador Shows How China Is Exerting Growing Power in America's Backyard," *NBC News*, September 4, 2021, https://www.nbcnews
.com/politics/national-security/project-el-salvador-shows-how-china
-exerting-growing-power-america-n1278464.

78. Andrew Katz, "State of Ruin," *Time*, https://web.archive.org/web/
20230409205641/https://time.com/venezuela-photographers/.

79. Angus Berwick, "How ZTE Helps Venezuela Create China-Style
Social Control," Reuters, November 14, 2018, https://www.reuters
.com/investigates/special-report/venezuela-zte/.

80. Leland Lazarus and Evan Ellis, "How China Helps the Cuban Regime
Stay Afloat and Shut Down Protests," *Diplomat*, August 3, 2021,
https://thediplomat.com/2021/08/how-china-helps-the-cuban-re
gime-stay-afloat-and-shut-down-protests/.

81. Benjamin R. Young, "Venezuela Is Becoming a Chinese and Russian
Cyber Hub on America's Doorstep," *National Interest*, June 27, 2022,
https://nationalinterest.org/blog/techland-when-great-power-com
petition-meets-digital-world/venezuela-becoming-chinese-and.

82. Gina Maka'a, "Solomon Islands Politician Critical of China Relations Ousted as Malaita Premier," Radio Free Asia, February 7, 2023,
https://www.rfa.org/english/news/pacific/malaita-premier-0207
2023004025.html.

83. For text of the communique banning PRC investment, see tweet
from Cleo Paskal, November 28, 2021, https://twitter.com/Cleo
Paskal/status/1465130915588419595. (Note: Since accessing this
link, Twitter.com was subsequently renamed X.com, and "tweets" were
renamed "posts.")

84. Gina Maka'a, "Solomon Islands Province Rejects Chinese Mobile Tow-
ers," Radio Free Asia, November 1, 2022, https://www.rfa.org/english/
news/china/solomons_huawei-11012022123951.html.

85. See Paskal, "Taiwan Does What Needs to Be Done."

86. Kynge, "China's Blueprint for an Alternative World Order."

CHAPTER 4. AMERICA'S TRIUMPHALIST HANGOVER

1. Charles Krauthammer, "The Unipolar Moment," *Foreign Affairs*, January 1, 1990, https://www.foreignaffairs.com/articles/1990-01-01/unipolar-moment.

2. Reid J. Epstein, "Kerry: Russia Behaving Like It's the 19th Century," *Politico*, March 2, 2014, https://www.politico.com/blogs/politico-now/2014/03/kerry-russia-behaving-like-its-the-19th-century-184280.

3. Epstein, "Kerry: Russia Behaving Like It's the 19th Century."

4. David Jackson, "Republicans Hit Obama Foreign Policy over Ukraine," *USA Today*, March 2, 2014, https://www.usatoday.com/story/theoval/2014/03/02/obama-russia-putin-ukraine-crimea/5944265/.

5. Jackson.

6. Antony J. Blinken, "The Administration's Approach to the People's Republic of China," U.S. Department of State, May 26, 2022, https://www.state.gov/the-administrations-approach-to-the-peoples-republic-of-china/.

7. Joseph R. Biden, "Remarks by President Biden before the 76th Session of the United Nations General Assembly," White House, September 21, 2021, https://www.whitehouse.gov/briefing-room/speeches-remarks/2021/09/21/remarks-by-president-biden-before-the-76th-session-of-the-united-nations-general-assembly/.

8. Author interview with Senator Ted Cruz (R-TX), "Peace through Strength," *Great Power Podcast*, December 14, 2021, https://podcasts.apple.com/us/podcast/great-power-podcast/id1593214289?i=1000544858005.

9. Jerry Dunleavy, "After Holding Out, Biden Administration Acknowledges Ongoing Uyghur Genocide in China That 'Cannot Be Ignored,'" *Washington Examiner*, March 10, 2021, https://www.washingtonexaminer.com/news/biden-administration-acknowledges-genocide-uyghurs-china-cannot-be-ignored.

10. Josh Rogin, "We Can't Fight Climate Change Using Forced Labor in China," *Washington Post*, June 24, 2021, https://www.washingtonpost.com/opinions/2021/06/24/china-solar-panels-biden-ban-uyghurs-human-rights/.

11. "China Puts Forward Two Lists during Talks with Visiting U.S. Deputy Secretary of State," Xinhua, July 26, 2021, http://www.xinhuanet.com/english/2021-07/26/c_1310087197.htm.

12. Josh Rogin, "Congress Needs to Act on Xi Jinping's Genocide Now," *Washington Post*, December 2, 2021, https://www.washingtonpost.com/opinions/2021/12/02/congress-needs-act-xi-jinpings-genocide-now/.

13. "U.S. Lawmakers Ask Biden Administration Why Some China Solar Giants Left off Slave Labor List," Reuters, July 12, 2022, https://www.reuters.com/legal/government/us-lawmakers-ask-biden-administration-why-some-china-solar-giants-left-off-slave-2022-07-12/.

14. Jimmy Quinn, "State Department Suddenly Uneasy Using the Term 'Malign Influence' to Call Out China," *National Review*, November 12, 2021, https://www.nationalreview.com/2021/11/state-department-suddenly-uneasy-using-the-term-malign-influence-to-call-out-china/.

15. Humeyra Pamuk, Michael Martina, and David Brunnstrom, "The Curious Case of a Map and a Disappearing Taiwan Minister at U.S. Democracy Summit," Reuters, December 13, 2021, https://www.reuters.com/world/asia-pacific/curious-case-map-disappearing-taiwan-minister-us-democracy-summit-2021-12-12/.

16. Demetri Sevastopulo, Richard Milne, Kathrin Hille, and Henry Foy, "US Wades into Spat between China and Lithuania over Taiwanese Office," *Financial Times*, January 20, 2022, https://www.ft.com/content/e646155d-6d8c-482a-8dfb-e4ef7d081bd8.

17. Demetri Sevastopulo and Kathrin Hille, "Nancy Pelosi to Visit Taiwan Next Month amid China Tensions," *Financial Times*, July 19, 2022, https://www.ft.com/content/09669099-1565-4723-86c9-84e0ca465825.

18. Peter Martin, Jenny Leonard, and Jennifer Jacobs, "From China to Big Sky: The Balloon That Unnerved the White House," February 3, 2023, https://www.bloomberg.com/news/articles/2023-02-04/from-china-to-big-sky-the-balloon-that-unnerved-the-white-house?leadSource=uverify%20wall.

19. Phelim Kine, "China Watcher: State's June 4 Snafu—Indo-Pacific Task Force—Congressional Tweets," *Politico*, June 8, 2023, https://www.politico.eu/newsletter/china-watcher/states-june-4-snafu-indo-pacific-task-force-congressional-tweets/.

20. Demetri Sevastopulo, "Antony Blinken to Visit China This Month in Sign of Easing Tensions," *Financial Times*, June 7, 2023, https://www.ft.com/content/f2a3ccf6-6019-4497-9b9e-0ff08d75455e.

21. Michael Martina, "Insight: Why the US Delayed China Sanctions after Shooting Down a Spy Balloon," Reuters, May 11, 2023, https://www

.reuters.com/world/us/why-us-delayed-china-sanctions-after-shoot ing-down-spy-balloon-2023–05–11/.

22. Daniel Currell, "Foreign Money in U.S. Universities Part III—Examining the Tangled Mess," National Security Institute, September 23, 2021, https://thescif.org/how-did-we-get-into-this-mess-foreign-mon ey-in-u-s-universities-part-i-2a7b3c15cb94.

23. Rush Doshi, *The Long Game: China's Grand Strategy to Displace American Order* (Oxford: Oxford University Press, 2021), 316.

24. Doshi, 316.

25. Nicholas A. Robinson and Gary R. Waxmonsky, "The U.S.-U.S.S.R. Agreement to Protect the Environment: 15 Years of Cooperation," *Environmental Law* 18, no. 403 (1988), http://digitalcommons.pace.edu/ lawfaculty/384/.

26. Dóra Vargha, *Polio across the Iron Curtain: Hungary's Cold War with an Epidemic* (Cambridge: Cambridge University Press, 2018), chapter 5 ("Sabin Saves the Day").

27. Vargha.

28. See chapter 6.

29. Carolyn Y. Johnson, Cate Cadell, and Joel Achenbach, "How China's Vaccine Strategy Stoked Its Looming 'Zero Covid' Crisis," *Washington Post*, December 1, 2022, https://www.washingtonpost.com/health/ 2022/12/01/china-zero-covid-vaccines/.

30. Roald Sagdeev and Susan Eisenhower, "United States-Soviet Space Cooperation during the Cold War," National Aeronautics and Space Administration, May 28, 2008, https://www.nasa.gov/50th/50th_ magazine/coldWarCoOp.html.

31. Sagdeev and Eisenhower.

32. See Rebecca Falconer, "U.S. Blocks Cotton Imports from China's Xinjiang Region over Forced Labor," *Axios*, December 2, 2020, https:// www.axios.com/2020/12/03/us-bans-cotton-imports-xinjiang-china -forced-labor.

33. See Alix Kroeger, "Xinjiang Cotton: How Do I Know If It's in My Jeans?," BBC, March 26, 2021, https://www.bbc.com/news/world -asia-china-56535822.

34. Marsha Blackburn (@MarshaBlackburn), "Thank you @realDonald Trump for banning cotton produced by forced Uyghur labor," Twitter, December 3, 2020, 6:08 a.m., https://twitter.com/MarshaBlackburn/ status/1334469578454392834?s=20.

35. Marsha Blackburn (@MarshaBlackburn), "China has a 5,000 year history of cheating and stealing," Twitter, December 3, 2020, 8:52 a.m., https://twitter.com/MarshaBlackburn/status/1334510812552163328?s=20.

36. Chen Weihua, "If China's Diplomats Are 'Wolf Warriors,' What Is Pompeo?" *China Daily*, December 11, 2020, https://www.chinadaily.com.cn/a/202012/11/WS5fd2b457a31024ad0ba9b229.html.

37. See Jeff Stein, Carol D. Leonnig, Josh Dawsey, and Garry Shih, "U.S. Officials Crafting Retaliatory Actions against China over Coronavirus as President Trump Fumes," *Washington Post*, April 30, 2020, https://www.washingtonpost.com/business/2020/04/30/trump-china-coronavirus-retaliation/.

38. For congressional support, see Doug Palmer, "Hawley Presses for Vote to Withdraw U.S. from the WTO," *Politico*, May 7, 2020, https://www.politico.com/news/2020/05/07/josh-hawley-us-withdraw-wto-243681. For President Trump's support, see Christine Wang, "Trump Threatens to Withdraw from World Trade Organization," *CNBC*, August 30, 2018, https://www.cnbc.com/2018/08/30/trump-threatens-to-withdraw-from-world-trade-organization.html.

39. See, in particular, the CHIPS and Science Act (Pub. L. No. 117–167, 136 Stat. 1366 [2022]).

40. See Jim Garamone, "U.S. Outlines Asia-Pacific Maritime Security Strategy," *DOD News*, August 21, 2015, https://www.defense.gov/News/News-Stories/Article/Article/614488/us-outlines-asia-pacific-maritime-security-strategy/.

41. H.R. 302–2 Division F—Build Act of 2018, https://www.dfc.gov/sites/default/files/2019-08/BILLS-115hr302_BUILDAct2018.pdf.

42. "Corker-Coons BUILD Act to Become Law," Ranking Member's Press Release, Senate Foreign Relations Committee, October 3, 2018, https://www.foreign.senate.gov/press/rep/release/corker-coons-build-act-to-become-law.

43. "China's 'Belt and Road' Strategy Has a New Competitor—Enter America's 'Blue Dot Network,'" Australian Broadcast Corporation, November 5, 2019, https://www.abc.net.au/news/2019-11-06/us-introduces-blue-dot-network-as-answer-to-belt-and-road/11675226.

44. Ben Kesling and Jon Emont, "U.S. Goes on the Offensive against China's Empire-Building Funding Plan," *Wall Street Journal*, April 9, 2019, https://www.wsj.com/articles/u-s-goes-on-the-offensive-against-chinas-empire-building-megaplan-11554809402.

45. OECD, *The Blue Dot Network: A Proposal for a Global Certification Framework for Quality Infrastructure Investment*, 2022, p. 18, https://www.oecd.org/daf/blue-dot-network-proposal-certification.pdf.

46. Ilan Berman, "In the War for Global Opinion, China Is Winning," *Newsweek*, September 20, 2022, https://www.newsweek.com/war-global-opinion-china-winning-opinion-1744007.

47. "Fact Sheet: President Biden and G7 Leaders Launch Build Back Better World (B3W) Partnership," Press Release, White House, June 12, 2021, https://www.whitehouse.gov/briefing-room/statements-releases/2021/06/12/fact-sheet-president-biden-and-g7-leaders-launch-build-back-better-world-b3w-partnership/.

48. "Fact Sheet: President Biden and G7 Leaders Launch Build Back Better World (B3W) Partnership."

49. "Fact Sheet: President Biden and G7 Leaders Formally Launch the Partnership for Global Infrastructure and Investment," Press Release, White House, June 26, 2022, https://www.whitehouse.gov/briefing-room/statements-releases/2022/06/26/fact-sheet-president-biden-and-g7-leaders-formally-launch-the-partnership-for-global-infrastructure-and-investment/.

50. Letter from Ranking Member James E. Risch to the Honorable Dev Jagadesan, Senate Foreign Relations Committee, October 29, 2021, https://www.foreign.senate.gov/imo/media/doc/211029%20-%20TO%20DFC%20-%20Dev%20Jagadesan%20-%20Solar%20letter.pdf.

51. Private meeting with diplomatic officials from a central Asian government, October 2022.

52. Author interview with Ilan Berman, "Disinformation, Misinformation, and 'Fake News,'" *Great Power Podcast*, December 21, 2022, https://podcasts.apple.com/us/podcast/great-power-podcast/id1593214289?i=1000590918464.

53. Author interview with Ilan Berman.

54. Quoted in Richard Rumelt, *Good Strategy, Bad Strategy: The Difference and Why It Matters* (New York: Crown Business, 2011), 28.

55. Thomas G. Mahnken, ed., *Net Assessment and Military Strategy: Retrospective and Prospective Essays* (New York: Cambria Press, 2020), 6.

56. Gordon Barrass, "U.S. Competitive Strategy during the Cold War," in *Competitive Strategies for the 21st Century: Theory, History, and Practice*, ed. Thomas G. Mahnken (Stanford: Stanford Security Studies, 2012), 78.

57. Barrass, 80.

58. Barrass, 80.

59. Ronald Reagan, *Ronald Reagan: An American Life* (New York: Simon & Schuster, 1990), 237–38.

60. National Defense Budget Estimates for FY1985, Office of the Assistant Secretary of Defense (Comptroller), https://www.esd.whs.mil/Portals/54/Documents/FOID/Reading%20Room/Other/NationalDefenseBudgetstimates_FY1985_March1984.pdf.

61. Thomas G. Mahnken, *Technology and the American Way of War since 1945* (New York: Columbia University Press, 2008), 148–52.

CHAPTER 5. BLUNTING BEIJING'S EMPIRE

1. "Interview: Osama bin Laden," *Frontline*, PBS, May 1998, https://www.pbs.org/wgbh/pages/frontline/shows/binladen/who/interview.html.

2. President Bush's Second Inaugural Address, NPR, January 20, 2005, https://www.npr.org/templates/story/story.php?storyId=4460172.

3. Reinhold Niebuhr, *The Irony of American History* (Chicago: University of Chicago Press, 1952), 2.

4. "Bin Laden: Goal Is to Bankrupt U.S.," CNN, November 1, 2004, https://www.cnn.com/2004/WORLD/meast/11/01/binladen.tape/.

5. *The 9/11 Commission Report: Final Report of the National Commission on Terrorist Attacks upon the United States*, July 22, 2004, p. 169, https://www.9-11commission.gov/report/911Report.pdf.

6. Neta C. Crawford, "The U.S. Budgetary Costs of the Post-9/11 Wars," Watson Institute: International & Public Affairs, Brown University, September 1, 2021, https://watson.brown.edu/costsofwar/files/cow/imce/papers/2021/Costs%20of%20War_U.S.%20Budgetary%20Costs%20of%20Post-9%2011%20Wars_9.1.21.pdf.

7. See Aaron Friedberg, *A Contest for Supremacy: China, America, and the Struggle for Mastery in Asia* (New York: W. W. Norton 2011), 131.

8. Friedberg, 131.

9. Friedberg, 131.

10. Friedberg, 131.

11. See Rush Doshi, *The Long Game: China's Grand Strategy to Displace American Order* (Oxford: Oxford University Press, 2021), 180.

12. Helene Cooper, "A Silver Lining to America's Waning Influence," *New York Times*, November 1, 2011, https://www.nytimes.com/2011/11/02/us/americas-waning-influence-has-a-silver-lining.html.

13. Tom Miller, *China's Asian Dream: Empire Building along the New Silk Road* (London: Zed Books, 2017), 248.

14. Eyck Freymann, *One Belt One Road: Chinese Power Meets the World* (Cambridge: Harvard University Press, 2020), 241.

15. Bruno Maçães, "A Preview of Your Chinese Future," *Foreign Policy*, December 7, 2018, https://foreignpolicy.com/2018/12/07/a-preview-of-your-chinese-future/.

16. Jonathan E. Hillman, *The Emperor's New Road: China and the Project of the Century* (New Haven: Yale University Press, 2020), 8.

17. Hillman, 15.

18. See Michael Schuman, *Superpower Interrupted: The Chinese History of the World* (New York: PublicAffairs, 2020), 88–89.

19. See Charles O. Hucker, *China's Imperial Past: An Introduction to Chinese History and Culture* (Stanford: Stanford University Press, 1975), 139.

20. Hucker, 139.

21. Schuman, *Superpower Interrupted*, 69.

22. Schuman, 74.

23. Schuman, 74.

24. See Schuman, 99, and René Grousset, *The Empire of the Steppes: A History of Central Asia*, trans. Naomi Walford (New Brunswick: Rutgers University Press, 1970), 119–20.

25. For an articulation of this perspective, see Hal Brands and Michael Beckley, *Danger Zone: The Coming Conflict with China* (New York: W. W. Norton, 2022).

26. Evelyn Cheng, "China's GDP Growth Misses Expectations in the Second Quarter," CNBC, July 14, 2022, https://www.cnbc.com/2022/07/15/china-q2-gdp.html.

27. "80% of CPEC Projects Worth $2 Billion Running Behind Schedule in Pakistan," *Times of India*, May 8, 2022, https://timesofindia.india times.com/world/pakistan/80-of-cpec-projects-worth-2-billion-run ning-behind-schedule-in-pakistan/articleshow/91419164.cms.

28. Ishaan Tharoor, "China Has a Hand in Sri Lanka's Economic Calamity," *Washington Post*, July 20, 2022, https://www.washingtonpost.com/world/2022/07/20/sri-lanka-china-debt-trap/.

29. See Ammar A. Malik, Bradley Parks, Brooke Russell, Joyce Jiahui Lin, Katherine Walsh, Kyra Solomon, Sheng Zhang, Thai-Binh Elston, and Seth Goodman, *Banking on the Belt and Road: Insights from a New*

Global Dataset of 13,427 Chinese Development Projects (Williamsburg, VA: AidData at William & Mary, 2021).

30. James Kynge, Kathrin Hille, Benjamin Parkin, and Jonathan Wheatley, "China Reckons with Its First Overseas Debt Crisis," *Financial Times*, July 21, 2022, https://www.ft.com/content/ccbe2b80-0c3e-4d58-a1 82-8728b443df9a.

31. Derek Scissors, "China Global Investment Tracker," American Enterprise Institute, https://www.aei.org/china-global-investment-tracker/.

32. Varg Folkman, "Italy Intends to Leave China's Belt and Road Initiative, Defense Minister Says," *Politico*, July 30, 2023, https://www.politico .eu/article/italy-leave-belt-and-road-initiative-china-minister-guido -crosetto/.

33. Sebastian Strangio, "Philippines Drops Chinese Funding For Three Railway Projects," *Diplomat*, October 27, 2023, https://thediplomat .com/2023/10/philippines-drops-chinese-funding-for-three-railway -projects/.

34. Xi Jinping, "Working Together to Deliver a Brighter Future for Belt and Road Cooperation," Second Belt and Road Forum for International Cooperation, April 26, 2019, http://www.beltandroadforum .org/english/n100/2019/0426/c22-1266.html.

35. Christina Lu, "China's Belt and Road to Nowhere," *Foreign Policy*, February 13, 2023, https://foreignpolicy.com/2023/02/13/china-belt -and-road-initiative-infrastructure-development-geopolitics/. See also James Kynge, "China's Blueprint for an Alternative World Order," *Financial Times*, August 23, 2023, https://www.ft.com/content/8ac52fe7 -e9db-48a8-b2f0-7305ab53f4c3.

36. Hillman.

37. Scissors, "China Global Investment Tracker."

38. Ian Easton, interview with Michael Sobolik, *Great Power Podcast*, August 3, 2022, https://podcasts.apple.com/us/podcast/great-power -podcast/id1593214289?i=1000574888457.

39. Bethany Allen-Ebrahimian, "China's Post-Reform Era Has Arrived— and Its Future Is Unclear," *Axios*, August 29, 2023, https://www.axios .com/2023/08/29/chinas-post-reform-era.

40. "Is This the End of Belt and Road, or Just the Beginning?" *ChinaFile*, April 24, 2019, https://www.chinafile.com/conversation/end-of-belt -and-road-or-just-beginning.

41. Nadège Rolland, *China's Eurasian Century? Political and Strategic Implications of the Belt and Road Initiative* (New Delhi: Pentagon Press, 2018), 156.

42. Gracia Watson, "Is America Ready for China's Belt and Road Challenge?" *National Interest*, March 29, 2021, https://nationalinterest.org/feature/america-ready-china's-belt-and-road-challenge-181421.

43. Matt Schrader and J. Michael Cole, "China Hasn't Given Up on the Belt and Road," *Foreign Affairs*, February 7, 2023, https://www.foreignaffairs.com/china/china-hasnt-given-up-on-belt-and-road.

44. Sheridan Prasso, "One of China's Most Ambitious Projects Becomes a Corridor to Nowhere," *Bloomberg*, March 2, 2020, https://www.bloomberg.com/news/features/2020-03-02/a-china-belt-and-road-project-becomes-a-corridor-to-nowhere#xj4y7vzkg.

45. Rolland, *China's Eurasian Century?* 173.

46. "One Belt One Road Documentary Episode One: Common Fate," CGTN, YouTube video, November 10, 2016, https://www.youtube.com/watch?v=_NtprkECCiU&t=2542s.

47. "One Belt One Road Documentary Episode One."

48. Author interview with Joshua Eisenman, "China and Africa," *Great Power Podcast*, April 22, 2022, https://podcasts.apple.com/us/podcast/great-power-podcast/id1593214289?i=1000558387096.

49. Ian Easton, *The Final Struggle: Inside China's Global Grand Strategy* (Manchester: Eastbridge Books, 2022), 191.

50. Ian Fleming, *Casino Royale* (London: Jonathan Cape, 1953).

51. For a comprehensive overview of the relationship between the United States and the Freely Associated States, see Michael Sobolik, "America's Strategic Play in the Pacific," *RealClearDefense*, November 24, 2020, https://www.realcleardefense.com/2020/11/24/americas_strategic_play_in_the_pacific_650799.html.

52. Ameya Paleja, "US to Build Over the Horizon Radar to Surveil the South China Sea," *Interesting Engineering*, January 2, 2023, https://interestingengineering.com/innovation/us-over-the-horizon-radar-palau.

53. See chapter 3.

54. "Treasury Sanctions Corrupt Actors in Africa and Asia," U.S. Department of Treasury, December 9, 2020, https://home.treasury.gov/news/press-releases/sm1206.

55. TACMOR radars require two ground locations: a transmit site and a receiving site. Had Wan Kuok Koi succeeded in establishing a special

economic zone on Palau's Angaur Island, he would have blocked the Pentagon from establishing the receiving site. See Bernadette Carreon, Aubrey Belford, and Martin Young, "Pacific Gambit: Inside the Chinese Communist Party and Triad Push into Palau," Organized Crime and Corruption Reporting Project, December 12, 2022, https://www.occrp.org/en/investigations/pacific-gambit-inside-the-chinese-communist-party-and-triad-push-into-palau. For background on the Department of Defense's plans to build the receiving site on Angaur Island, see "REQUEST FOR PROPOSAL: N62742-22-R-1322, PAF 198127 TACMOR UTILITIES AND INFRASTRUCTURE SUPPORT," Naval Facilities Engineering Systems Command Pacific, https://imlive.s3.amazonaws.com/Federal%20Government/ID20900 37852453722601393022988208048552753/N62742-22-R-1322%20 Front%20End.pdf.

56. "U.S. Blacklists Chinese Crime Boss, Others in Anti-Corruption Sanctions," Reuters, December 9, 2020, https://www.reuters.com/article/us-usa-china-sanctions/u-s-blacklists-chinese-crime-boss-others-in-anti-corruption-sanctions-idUSKBN28J267.

57. "Treasury Sanctions Corrupt Actors in Africa and Asia," U.S. Department of Treasury.

58. Kenneth Tee, "IGP: Fugitive Businessman Nicky Liow Had Ties with Ex-Macau Triad Leader 'Broken Tooth' Wan Kuok-koi," Malay-Mail, March 30, 2021, https://www.malaymail.com/news/malaysia/2021/03/30/igp-fugitive-businessman-nicky-liow-had-ties-with-ex-macau-triad-leader-bro/1962419.

59. Shelley K. Mesch, "Air Force Moving Forward with TACMOR Radar System," Inside Defense, October 12, 2023, https://insidedefense.com/insider/air-force-moving-forward-tacmor-radar-system.

60. "Why China's Belt & Road Initiative Faces Overwhelming Odds in Its Fight against Corruption," AML RightSource, May 6, 2021, https://www.arachnys.com/why-chinas-belt-road-initiative-faces-overwhelming-odds-in-its-fight-against-corruption/.

61. "Internationally Scandal-Tainted Chinese Company Working on Second Yangon Project," Irrawaddy, October 25, 2019, https://www.irrawaddy.com/news/burma/internationally-scandal-tainted-chinese-company-working-second-yangon-project.html.

62. "U.S. Imposes Restrictions on Certain PRC State-Owned Enterprises and Executives for Malign Activities in the South China Sea,"

U.S. Embassy in Costa Rica, Press Release, August 26, 2020, https://cr.usembassy.gov/pr200826-prc/.

63. Office of the Secretary of Defense, *Military and Security Developments Involving the People's Republic of China 2021: Annual Report to Congress*, Department of Defense, pp. 131–32, https://media.defense.gov/2021/Nov/03/2002885874/-1/-1/0/2021-CMPR-FINAL.PDF.

64. For background on the UAE gambit, see Gordon Lubold and Warren P. Strobel, "Secret Chinese Port Project in Persian Gulf Rattles U.S. Relations with U.A.E.," *Wall Street Journal*, November 19, 2021, https://www.wsj.com/articles/us-china-uae-military-11637274224. For China's port access in the Solomon Islands, see Kirsty Needham, "EXCLUSIVE Solomon Islands Considers Security Cooperation with China—Official," Reuters, March 24, 2022, https://www.reuters.com/world/exclusive-solomon-islands-considers-security-cooperation-with-china-official-2022-03-24/. For Beijing's overtures to Equatorial Guinea, see Michael M. Phillips, "China Seeks First Military Base on Africa's Atlantic Coast, U.S. Intelligence Finds," *Wall Street Journal*, December 5, 2021, https://www.wsj.com/articles/china-seeks-first-military-base-on-africas-atlantic-coast-u-s-intelligence-finds-11638726327.

65. Phelim Kine, "U.S. Turns the Screws on Solomon Islands to Counter China," *Politico*, April 28, 2022, https://www.politico.com/newsletters/politico-china-watcher/2022/04/28/u-s-turns-the-screws-on-solomon-islands-to-counter-china-00028449.

66. Daniel J. Kritenbrink, "Teleconference with Assistant Secretary of State for East Asian and Pacific Affairs Daniel Kritenbrink," U.S. Department of State, April 26, 2022, https://www.state.gov/teleconference-with-assistant-secretary-of-state-for-east-asian-and-pacific-affairs-daniel-kritenbrink/.

67. Georgia Hitch, "Scott Morrison Says Chinese Military Base in Solomon Islands Would Be 'Red Line' for Australia, US," *Australia Broadcast Corporation*, April 23, 2022, https://www.abc.net.au/news/2022-04-24/scott-morrison-china-naval-base-solomon-islands-red-line/101011710.

68. Kate Lyons and Dorothy Wickham, "The Deal That Shocked the World: Inside the China-Solomons Security Pact," *Guardian*, April 20, 2022, https://www.theguardian.com/world/2022/apr/20/the-deal-that-shocked-the-world-inside-the-china-solomons-security-pact.

69. U.S. Embassy in Mauritius & Seychelles, https://mu.usembassy.gov/embassy-vpp/seychelles/.

70. On land seizures, see "China's Plans in Myanmar at Odds with Local Expectations," Voice of America, November 11, 2016, https://www.voanews.com/a/chinas-plans-for-myanmar-local-expections-at-odd/3591981.html. On employment, see Scott Morris, "The Kunming-Vientiane Railway: The Economic, Procurement, Labor, and Safeguards Dimensions of a Chinese Belt and Road Project," Center for Global Development, May 2019, https://data.opendevelopment mekong.net/dataset/8399d692-327b-43df-ae9c-4ea4ad5d8a20/resource/eccdfe62-13cb-4884-25e-a0e4a417c83f/download/kun ming-vientiane-railway-economic-procurement-labor-and-safe guards-dimensions-chinese.pdf. For a broader look at Chinese labor and BRI projects, see Jennifer Hillman and Alex Tippett, "Who Built That? Labor and the Belt and Road Initiative," Council on Foreign Relations, July 6, 2021, https://www.cfr.org/blog/who-built-labor-and-belt-and-road-initiative.

71. "WWF and Greening the Belt and Road Initiative," World Wildlife Foundation, November 2, 2017, https://www.wwf.org.hk/en/?19680/Feature-Story-WWF-and-Greening-the-Belt-and-Road-Initiative.

72. Drake Long, "Experts Raise Alarm over Destruction of Coral Reefs in South China Sea," Radio Free Asia, October 5, 2020, https://www.rfa.org/english/news/china/southchinsea-coral-10052020190143.html.

73. Sébastian Seibt, "Djibouti-China Marriage 'Slowly Unravelling' as Investment Project Disappoints," France24, April 9, 2021, https://www.france24.com/en/africa/20210409-djibouti-china-marriage-slowly-unravelling-as-investment-project-disappoints.

74. Craig Singleton, interview with Michael Sobolik, *Great Power Podcast*, November 21, 2022, https://podcasts.apple.com/us/podcast/great-power-podcast/id1593214289?i=1000587006442.

75. Bureau of Public Affairs, Special Report No. 88, "Soviet 'Active' Measures: Forgery, Disinformation, Political Operations," U.S. Department of State, October 1981, https://www.hsdl.org/?view&did=807615.

76. Fletcher Schoen and Christopher J. Lamb, "Deception, Disinformation, and Strategic Communications: How One Interagency Group Made a Major Difference," Institute for National Strategic Studies, June 2012, p. 101, https://ndupress.ndu.edu/Portals/68/Documents/stratperspec tive/inss/Strategic-Perspectives-11.pdf.

77. Ilan Berman, interview with Michael Sobolik, *Great Power Podcast*, December 21, 2022, https://podcasts.apple.com/us/podcast/great-power-podcast/id1593214289?i=1000590918464.

78. Berman, interview with Sobolik.

CHAPTER 6. TESTING RED LINES

1. For background on Carl von Ossietzky and the political persecution he endured, see "Carl von Ossietzky," The Nobel Prize, https://www.nobelprize.org/prizes/peace/1935/ossietzky/facts/.

2. Pete Walker, "Nobel Peace Prize Placed on Empty Chair in Honor of Liu Xiaobo," *Guardian*, December 10, 2010, https://www.theguardian.com/world/2010/dec/10/nobel-peace-prize-liu-xiaobo.

3. "China Cries Foul over Peace Prize," France24, October 8, 2010, https://www.france24.com/en/20101008-china-cries-foul-over-nobel-peace-prize-liu-xiaobo.

4. "China Cries Foul."

5. "China Cries Foul."

6. Christopher Bodeen, "Norway Snub Shows Sharp Edge of Chinese Diplomacy," AP, October 28, 2013, https://apnews.com/article/9ba1a4b603f54a3ca24252336517def6.

7. Barack H. Obama, "Statement on the Awarding of the Nobel Peace Prize to Liu Xiaobo," December 10, 2010, https://www.govinfo.gov/content/pkg/DCPD-201001059/pdf/DCPD-201001059.pdf.

8. Barack H. Obama and Xi Jinping, "Press Conference with President Obama and President Hu of the People's Republic of China," White House, January 19, 2011, https://obamawhitehouse.archives.gov/the-press-office/2011/01/19/press-conference-president-obama-and-president-hu-peoples-republic-china.

9. "Charter 08," December 10, 2008, https://www.cecc.gov/resources/legal-provisions/charter-08-chinese-and-english-text.

10. "Charter 08."

11. Sen. Ted Cruz (@SenTedCruz), "This man belongs to history," Twitter, October 19, 2017, 10:41 a.m., https://twitter.com/SenTedCruz/status/921038632772931585?s=20.

12. Masashi Crete-Nishihata, Jeffrey Knockel, Blake Miller, Jason Q. Ng, Lotus Ruan, Lokman Tsui, and Ruohan Xiong, "Remembering Liu Xiaobo: Analyzing Censorship of the Death of Liu Xiaobo on WeChat and Weibo," Citizen Lab, June 16, 2017, https://citizenlab

.ca/2017/07/analyzing-censorship-of-the-death-of-liu-xiaobo-on
-wechat-and-weibo/.

13. William J. Clinton, "Clinton on Firewall and Jello," C-SPAN, March 9, 2000, https://www.c-span.org/video/?c4893404/user-clip-clinton-fire wall-jello.

14. See Sean Roberts, "Why Did the United States Take China's Word on Supposed Uighur Terrorists?" *Foreign Policy*, November 10, 2020, https://foreignpolicy.com/2020/11/10/why-did-the-united-states -take-chinas-word-on-supposed-uighur-terrorists/.

15. David J. Lynch, "Trump Says He Might Veto Legislation That Aims to Protect Human Rights in Hong Kong because Bill Could Affect China Trade Talks," *Washington Post*, November 22, 2019, https://www. washingtonpost.com/business/2019/11/22/trump-says-he-might -veto-legislation-that-aims-protect-human-rights-hong-kong-because -bill-would-impact-china-trade-talks/.

16. "Authorizing Extension of Nondiscriminatory Treatment (Normal Trade Relations Treatment) to People's Republic of China," Cong. Rec. vol. 146, no. 65, May 23, 2000, https://www.congress.gov/congressio nal-record/volume-146/issue-65/house-section/article/H3596-%20 2?q=%7B%22search%22%3A%5B%22h.r.4444%22%2C%22h.r.4444 %22%5D%7D&amp%3Bs=9&amp%3Br=8.

17. "To Authorize Extension of Nondiscriminatory Treatment to the People's Republic of China—Motion to Proceed," Cong. Rec. vol. 146, no. 100, July 27, 2000, https://www.congress.gov/congressional -record/volume-146/issue-100/senate-section/article/S7768-%20 2?q=%7B%22search%22%3A%5B%22H.R.4444%22%2C%22H.R.4 444%22%5D%7D&amp%3Bs=4&amp%3Br=+39.

18. James Seng, Global Information Infrastructure Commission, http:// giic.org/commissioners/james-seng_/.

19. Vassily Aksyonov, "Sakharov Plaza," *Washington Post*, March 15, 1987, https://www.washingtonpost.com/archive/opinions/1987/03/15/ sakharov-plaza/afb0341e-5205-4692-8810-c1ebcbe3197d/.

20. Josh Rogin, "How China Got a U.S. Senator to Do Its Political Bid-ding," *Washington Post*, December 17, 2017, https://www.washing tonpost.com/opinions/global-opinions/how-china-got-a-us-senator -to-do-its-political-bidding/2017/12/17/8eee82c6-e1dc-11e7-8679 -a9728984779c_story.html.

21. Congressional Record—Senate, November 4, 2015, https://www.con gress.gov/crec/2015/11/04/CREC-2015-11-04-pt1-PgS7743.pdf.

22. "Transcript: Interventionism vs. Isolationism: A Conversation with U.S. Sen. Ted Cruz," Hudson Institute, September 6, 2019, https://www.hudson.org/national-security-defense/transcript-intervention ism-vs-isolationism-a-conversation-with-u-s-sen-ted-cruz.

23. Private correspondence reviewed by author.

24. "'My Lobotomy': Howard Dully's Journey," *All Things Considered*, NPR, November 16, 2005, https://www.npr.org/2005/11/16/5014080/my -lobotomy-howard-dullys-journey.

25. See Congressional-Executive Commission on China, "Xinjiang," Annual Report 2021, https://www.cecc.gov/sites/chinacommission.house.gov/ files/documents/2021%20AR%20Xinjiang_0.pdf. The author's use of 'lobotomize' stems from a conversation with Nury Turkel, former Commissioner of the United States Commission on International Religious Freedom. See Nury Turkel, interview with Michael Sobolik, "The Uyghur Genocide," *Great Power Podcast*, May 11, 2022, https://podcasts.apple.com/us/podcast/great-power-podcast/id1593214289 ?i=1000560589161.

26. "'To Make Us Slowly Disappear': The Chinese Government's Assault on the Uyghurs," United States Holocaust Memorial Museum, November 2021, https://www.ushmm.org/m/pdfs/November_2021_Uyghur_ Report.pdf.

27. Convention on the Prevention and Punishment of the Crime of Genocide, December 9, 1948, https://treaties.un.org/doc/Publication/ MTDSG/Volume%20I/Chapter%20IV/IV-1.en.pdf.

28. For Pompeo's comments, see David Brunnstrom and Lesley Wroughton, "Pompeo Calls China's Treatment of Uighurs 'Stain of the Century,'" Reuters, July 18, 2019, https://www.reuters.com/article/us -usa-religion-china/pompeo-calls-chinas-treatment-of-uighurs -stain-of-the-century-idUSKCN1UD20P. For Biden's comments, see Remarks by President Biden at the Dedication of the Dodd Center for Human Rights, White House, Press Release, October 15, 2021, https://www.whitehouse.gov/briefing-room/statements-relea ses/2021/10/15/remarks-by-president-biden-at-the-dedication-of -the-dodd-center-for-human-rights/.

29. Bethany Allen-Ebrahimian, "U.S. Sanctions China's Paramilitary in Xinjiang," *Axios*, July 31, 2020, https://www.axios.com/2020/07/31/us-sanctions-china-paramilitary-xinjiang-xpcc.

30. See Xinjiang Supply China Business Advisory, U.S. Department of State, July 13, 2021, https://www.state.gov/xinjiang-supply-chain-business-advisory/.

31. Alex Willemyns, "Nearly $500 Million in US Imports Blocked Due to Uyghur Forced Labor," Radio Free Asia, March 15, 2023, https://www.rfa.org/english/news/uyghur/cbp-forced-labor-03152023113754.html.

32. Haley Byrd Wilt, "How the Uyghur Forced Labor Prevention Act Became Law," *Dispatch*, June 20, 2022, https://thedispatch.com/wp-content/uploads/2022/10/How-the-Uyghur-Forced-Labor-Prevention-Act-Became-Law-Final-Version.pdf.

33. See Michael Sobolik, "Primary Jurisdiction of Humanitarian Concern: A New Tool to Blunt China's Campaign in Xinjiang," American Foreign Policy Council, September 25, 2020, https://www.afpc.org/uploads/documents/IPSP_Memorandum_-_Xinjiang_FINAL_PAPER.pdf.

34. For possible risks, see Andreea Brinza, "Putin's War Has Killed China's Eurasian Railway Dreams," *Foreign Policy*, March 1, 2022, https://foreignpolicy.com/2022/03/01/belt-road-initiative-new-eurasian-land-bridge-china-russia-poland/.

35. "Xinjiang Aims for Financial Hub on Economic Belt," Xinhua, November 8, 2014, http://us.china-embassy.gov.cn/eng/zt/Xinjiang/201412/t20141202_4917317.htm.

36. Chris Buckley and Amy Qin, "China's Leader Visits Xinjiang for the First Time since Imposing Crackdown," *New York Times*, July 15, 2022, https://www.nytimes.com/2022/07/15/world/asia/china-xi-xinjiang.html.

37. For the Han dynasty's campaigns, see René Grousset, *The Empire of the Steppes: A History of Central Asia*, trans. Naomi Walford (New Brunswick: Rutgers University Press, 1970), 38–39, 44–45. For Tang dynasty campaigns, see Grousset, *Empire of the Steppes*, 99–101.

38. George W. Bush, "President Signs USA PATRIOT Act," October 26, 2001, https://georgewbush-whitehouse.archives.gov/news/releases/2001/10/images/20011026-5.html.

39. Juan Zarate, *Treasury's War: The Unleashing of a New Era of Financial Warfare* (New York: PublicAffairs, 2013), 151.

40. Rebecca M. Nelson and Martin A. Weiss, "The U.S. Dollar as the World's Dominant Reserve Currency," *Congressional Research Service*, September 15, 2022, https://crsreports.congress.gov/product/pdf/IF/IF11707.

41. "Li Wenliang's 'Admonishment Notice,'" *China Digital Times*, February 6, 2020, https://chinadigitaltimes.net/2020/02/translation-li-wenliangs-admonishment-notice/.

42. "Early and Combined Interventions Crucial in Tackling Covid-19 Spread in China," University of Southampton, March 11, 2020, https://www.southampton.ac.uk/news/2020/03/covid-19-china.page.

43. Sandip Sen, "How China Locked Down Internally for COVID-19, but Pushed Foreign Travel," *Economic Times*, April 30, 2020, https://economictimes.indiatimes.com/blogs/Whathappensif/how-china-locked-down-internally-for-covid-19-but-pushed-foreign-travel/.

44. Yanzhong Huang, "Is China Setting Itself Up for Another Epidemic?," *New York Times*, January 23, 2020, https://www.nytimes.com/2020/01/23/opinion/coronavirus-china-wuhan.html.

45. "Translation: Notes from an Account Bombing, by Mimiyana," *China Digital Times*, March 20, 2020, https://chinadigitaltimes.net/2020/03/translation-notes-from-an-account-bombing-by-mimiyana/.

46. WHO Coronavirus (COVID-19) Dashboard, World Health Organization, https://covid19.who.int.

47. Steven Lee Myers, "China Spins Tale That the U.S. Army Started the Coronavirus Epidemic," *New York Times*, March 13, 2020, https://www.nytimes.com/2020/03/13/world/asia/coronavirus-china-conspiracy-theory.html.

48. Becket Adams, "Yet Another Country Flags Cache of Defective Chinese-Manufactured Medical Equipment," *Washington Examiner*, April 7, 2020, https://www.washingtonexaminer.com/opinion/yet-another-country-flags-cache-of-defective-chinese-manufactured-medical-equipment.

49. Daphne Psaledakis and Simon Lewis, "U.S. Will Not Leave Australia Alone to Face China Coercion—Blinken," Reuters, May 13, 2021, https://www.reuters.com/world/asia-pacific/us-will-not-leave-australia-alone-face-china-coercion-blinken-2021-05-13/.

50. See Jon Pelson, *Wireless Wars: China's Dangerous Domination of 5G and How We're Fighting Back* (Dallas: BenBella Books, 2021), 49–58.

51. See Sarah Lai Stirland, "Cisco Leak: 'Great Firewall' of China Was a Chance to Sell More Routers," *Wired*, May 28, 2008, https://www.wired.com/2008/05/leaked-cisco-do/.

52. Sui-Lee Wee, "China Uses DNA to Track Its People, with the Help of American Expertise," *New York Times*, February 21, 2019, https://www.nytimes.com/2019/02/21/business/china-xinjiang-uighur-dna-thermo-fisher.html.

53. Steven Lee Myers, "Meta Removes Chinese Effort to Influence U.S. Elections," *New York Times*, September 27, 2022, https://www.nytimes.com/2022/09/27/technology/meta-chinese-influence-us-elections.html.

54. Haleluya Hadero, "Gap Grows between TikTok Users, Lawmakers on Potential Ban," AP, March 26, 2023, https://apnews.com/article/tiktok-ban-congress-hearing-bytedance-china-biden-ceo-a92f048762d6657f291affb7a0ce6386.

55. Corbin Smith, "Daryl Morey's Tweet on Hong Kong Shows How China Is Calling the Shots in the NBA," *NBC News*, October 8, 2019, https://www.nbcnews.com/think/opinion/daryl-morey-s-tweet-hong-kong-shows-how-china-calling-ncna1063551.

56. Kai Strittmater, *We Have Been Harmonized: Life in China's Surveillance State* (New York: Custom House, 2020), 99.

57. Strittmater, 100–101.

58. Strittmater, 99.

59. Strittmater, 103.

60. Josh Chin and Liza Lin, *Surveillance State: Inside China's Quest to Launch a New Era of Social Control* (New York: St. Martin's Press, 2020), 9.

61. See Josh Chin and Liza Lin, "The Two Faces of China's Surveillance State," *Wall Street Journal*, September 2, 2022, https://www.wsj.com/articles/the-two-faces-of-chinas-surveillance-state-11662130940.

62. See Ryan Fedasiuk, "Buying Silence: The Price of Internet Censorship in China," Jamestown Foundation, January 12, 2021, https://jamestown.org/program/buying-silence-the-price-of-internet-censorship-in-china/.

63. "Document 9: A ChinaFile Translation," *ChinaFile*, November 8, 2013, https://www.chinafile.com/document-9-chinafile-translation.

64. Wayne Ma, "Marriott Employee Roy Jones Hit 'Like.' Then China Got Mad," *Wall Street Journal*, March 3, 2018, https://www.wsj

.com/articles/marriott-employee-roy-jones-hit-like-then-china-got
-mad-1520094910.

65. Matt Pottinger, interview with Michael Sobolik, "Tearing Down the
    Great Firewall," *Great Power Podcast*, January 4, 2023, https://pod
    casts.apple.com/us/podcast/great-power-podcast/id1593214289
    ?i=1000592462741.

66. Bill Marczak, Nicholas Weaver, Jakub Dalek, Roya Ensafi, David
    Fifield, Sarah McKune, Arn Rey, John Scott-Railton, Ron Deibert,
    and Vern Paxson, "China's Great Cannon," CitizenLab, April 10, 2015,
    https://citizenlab.ca/2015/04/chinas-great-cannon/.

67. Ellen Nakashima, "Chinese Breach Data of 4 Million Federal Work-
    ers," *Washington Post*, June 4, 2015, https://www.washingtonpost.com/
    world/national-security/chinese-hackers-breach-federal-govern
    ments-personnel-office/2015/06/04/889c0e52-0af7-11e5-95fd-d5
    80f1c5d44e_story.html.

68. Eric Geller, "U.S., Allies Slam China for Brazen Cyberattacks as Trump
    Administration Indicts Hackers," *Politico*, December 20, 2018, https://
    www.politico.com/story/2018/12/20/trump-administration-us-allies
    -condemn-china-for-brazen-cyberattacks-1070984.

69. "How It Happened: Transcript of the US-China Opening Remarks
    in Alaska," *Nikkei Asia*, March 19, 2021, https://asia.nikkei.com/Pol
    itics/International-relations/US-China-tensions/How-it-happened
    -Transcript-of-the-US-China-opening-remarks-in-Alaska.

CONCLUSION

1. John Pomfret and Matt Pottinger, "Xi Jinping Says He Is Preparing
   China for War," *Foreign Affairs*, March 29, 2023, https://www.foreign
   affairs.com/united-states/xi-jinping-says-he-preparing-china-war.

2. For background on Global Magnitsky sanctions, see "FAQ: Global
   Magnitsky Sanctions," Department of Treasury, December 27, 2017,
   https://ofac.treasury.gov/media/8651/download?inline. For legal text,
   see National Defense Authorization Act for Fiscal Year 2017, Pub. L.
   No. 114–328, 130 Stat. 2000 (2016), Title XII, Subtitle F, https://
   www.congress.gov/114/plaws/publ328/PLAW-114publ328.pdf.

3. Rep. Mike Gallagher, "Chairman Gallagher's Opening Remarks," the
   Select Committee on the CCP, Press Release, February 28, 2023,
   https://selectcommitteeontheccp.house.gov/media/press-releases/
   chairman-gallaghers-opening-remarks.

SELECTED BIBLIOGRAPHY

Biden, Joseph R. "Remarks by President Biden before the 76th Session of the United Nations General Assembly." White House. September 21, 2021. https://www.whitehouse.gov/briefing-room/speeches-remarks/2021/09/21/remarks-by-president-biden-before-the-76th-session-of-the-united-nations-general-assembly/.

Blinken, Antony J. "The Administration's Approach to the People's Republic of China." U.S. Department of State. May 26, 2022. https://www.state.gov/the-administrations-approach-to-the-peoples-republic-of-china/.

Bloodworth, Dennis. *The Chinese Looking Glass.* New York: Farrar, Straus and Giroux, 1967.

Brands, Hal, and Michael Beckley. *Danger Zone: The Coming Conflict with China.* New York: W. W. Norton, 2022.

Brunnstrom, David, and Michael Martina. "Xi Denies China Turning Artificial Islands into Military Bases." Reuters, September 25, 2015. https://www.reuters.com/article/us-usa-china-pacific/xi-denies-china-turning-artificial-islands-into-military-bases-idUSKCN0RP1ZH20150925.

Bush, George H. W., and Brent Scowcroft. *A World Transformed.* New York: Vintage Books, 1998.

Chin, Josh, and Liza Lin. *Surveillance State: Inside China's Quest to Launch a New Era of Social Control.* New York: St. Martin's Press, 2020.

Crossley, Pamala K. *A Translucent Mirror: History and Identity in Qing Imperial Ideology.* Berkley: University of California Press, 1999.

Cruz, Ted. Interview with Michael Sobolik. "Peace through Strength." *Great Power Podcast.* December 14, 2021. https://podcasts.apple.com/us/podcast/great-power-podcast/id1593214289?i=1000544858005.

Doğan, Asım. *Hegemony with Chinese Characteristics: From the Tributary System to the Belt and Road Initiative.* New York: Routledge, 2021.

Doshi, Rush. *The Long Game: China's Grand Strategy to Displace American Order.* Oxford: Oxford University Press, 2021.

Easton, Ian. *The Final Struggle: Inside China's Global Grand Strategy*. Manchester: Eastbridge Books, 2022.

———. Interview with Michael Sobolik. "The Ideology of the Chinese Communist Party." *Great Power Podcast*. August 3, 2022. https://podcasts.apple.com/us/podcast/great-power-podcast/id1593214289?i=1000574888457.

Eisenman, Joshua. Interview with Michael Sobolik. "China and Africa." *Great Power Podcast*. April 22, 2022. https://podcasts.apple.com/us/podcast/great-power-podcast/id1593214289?i=1000558387096.

Epstein, Reid J. "Kerry: Russia Behaving Like It's the 19th Century." *Politico*, March 2, 2024. https://www.politico.com/blogs/politico-now/2014/03/kerry-russia-behaving-like-its-the-19th-century-184280.

French, Howard W. *Everything under the Heavens: How the Past Helps Shape China's Push for Global Power*. New York: Vintage Books, 2018.

Freymann, Eyck. *One Belt One Road: Chinese Power Meets the World*. Cambridge: Harvard University Press, 2021.

Friedberg, Aaron. *A Contest for Supremacy: China, America, and the Struggle for Mastery in Asia*. New York: W. W. Norton, 2011.

Fukuyama, Francis. "The End of History?" *National Interest* 16 (Summer 1989): 3–18.

Grousset, René. *The Empire of the Steppes: A History of Central Asia*. Translated by Naomi Walford. New Brunswick: Rutgers University Press, 1970.

Hillman, Jonathan E. *The Emperor's New Road: China and the Project of the Century*. New Haven: Yale University Press, 2020.

Hucker, Charles O. *China's Imperial Past: An Introduction to Chinese History and Culture*. Stanford: Stanford University Press, 1975.

Johnston, Alastair I. *Cultural Realism: Strategic Culture and Grand Strategy in Chinese History*. Princeton: Princeton University Press, 1995.

Kang, David. *East Asia before the West: Five Centuries of Trade and Tribute*. New York: Columbia University Press, 2012.

Kissinger, Henry. *On China*. New York: Penguin Press, 2011.

Latourette, Kenneth S. *The Chinese: Their History and Culture*. New York: Macmillan, 1964.

Lu, Christina. "China's Belt and Road to Nowhere." *Foreign Policy*, February 13, 2023. https://foreignpolicy.com/2023/02/13/china-belt-and-road-initiative-infrastructure-development-geopolitics/.

Mackinder, Sir Halford J. *Democratic Ideals and Reality: A Study in the Politics of Reconstruction*. New York: Henry Holt, 1919.

Mahnken, Thomas G., ed. *Competitive Strategies for the 21st Century: Theory, History, and Practice.* Stanford: Stanford University Press, 2012.

———. *Net Assessment and Military Strategy: Retrospective and Prospective Essays.* New York: California Press, 2020.

Martina, Michael. "Insight: Why the US Delayed China Sanctions after Shooting down a Spy Balloon." Reuters, May 11, 2023. https://www.reuters.com/world/us/why-us-delayed-china-sanctions-after-shooting-down-spy-balloon-2023-05-11/.

Nakashima, Ellen, and Cate Cadell. "China Secretly Building Naval Facility in Cambodia, Western Officials Say." *Washington Post*, June 6, 2022. https://www.washingtonpost.com/national-security/2022/06/06/cambodia-china-navy-base-ream/.

Needham, Kirsty. "EXCLUSIVE Solomon Islands Considers Security Cooperation with China—Official." Reuters, March 24, 2022. https://www.reuters.com/world/exclusive-solomon-islands-considers-security-cooperation-with-china-official-2022-03-24/.

Neibuhr, Reinhold. *The Irony of American History.* Chicago: University of Chicago Press, 1952.

Obama, Barack H. "Statement on the Awarding of the Nobel Peace Prize to Liu Xiaobo." December 10, 2010. https://www.govinfo.gov/content/pkg/DCPD-201001059/pdf/DCPD-201001059.pdf.

Pelson, Jon. *Wireless Wars: China's Dangerous Domination of 5G and How We're Fighting Back.* Dallas: BenBella Books, 2021.

Pomfret, John, and Matt Pottinger. "Xi Jinping Says He Is Preparing China for War." *Foreign Affairs*, March 29, 2023. https://www.foreignaffairs.com/united-states/xi-jinping-says-he-preparing-china-war.

Pompeo, Michael R. "Determination of the Secretary of State on Atrocities in Xinjiang." Department of State, January 19, 2021. https://2017-2021.state.gov/determination-of-the-secretary-of-state-on-atrocities-in-xinjiang/index.html.

Pottinger, Matthew. Interview with Michael Sobolik. "Tearing Down the Great Firewall." *Great Power Podcast.* January 4, 2023. https://podcasts.apple.com/us/podcast/great-power-podcast/id1593214289?i=1000592462741.

Pottinger, Matthew, Matthew Johnson, and David Feith. "Xi Jinping in His Own Words: What China's Leader Wants—and How to Stop Him from Getting It." *Foreign Affairs*, November, 30, 2022. https://www.foreignaffairs.com/china/xi-jinping-his-own-words.

Prasso, Sheridan. "One of China's Most Ambitious Projects Becomes a Corridor to Nowhere." *Bloomberg*, March 2, 2020. https://www.bloomberg.com/news/features/2020-03-02/a-china-belt-and-road-project-becomes-a-corridor-to-nowhere#xj4y7vzkg.

Reagan, Ronald. *Ronald Reagan: An American Life*. New York: Simon & Schuster, 1990.

Roberts, Sean. "Why Did the United States Take China's Word on Supposed Uighur Terrorists?" *Foreign Policy*, November 10, 2020. https://foreignpolicy.com/2020/11/10/why-did-the-united-states-take-chinas-word-on-supposed-uighur-terrorists/.

Rogin, Josh. *Chaos under Heaven: Trump, Xi, and the Battle for the 21st Century*. New York: Houghton Mifflin Harcourt, 2021.

———. "Congress Needs to Act on Xi Jinping's Genocide Now." *Washington Post*, December 2, 2021. https://www.washingtonpost.com/opinions/2021/12/02/congress-needs-act-xi-jinpings-genocide-now/.

———. "How China Got a U.S. Senator to Do Its Political Bidding." *Washington Post*, December 17, 2017. https://www.washingtonpost.com/opinions/global-opinions/how-china-got-a-us-senator-to-do-its-political-bidding/2017/12/17/8eee82c6-e1dc-11e7-8679-a9728984779c_story.html.

Rolland, Nadège. *China's Eurasian Century? Political and Strategic Implications of the Belt and Road Initiative*. New Delhi: Pentagon Press, 2018.

Schrader, Matt, and J. Michael Cole. "China Hasn't Given Up on the Belt and Road." *Foreign Affairs*, February 7, 2023. https://www.foreignaffairs.com/china/china-hasnt-given-belt-and-road.

Schuman, Michael. Interview with Michael Sobolik. "China's Strategic Culture." *Great Power Podcast*. November 29, 2021. https://spotifyanchor-web.app.link/e/Fd2qmVvZcub.

———. *Superpower Interrupted: The Chinese History of the World*. New York: PublicAffairs, 2020.

Scissors, Derek. "China Global Investment Tracker." American Enterprise Institute. https://www.aei.org/china-global-investment-tracker/.

Sevastopulo, Demetri, and Kathrin Hille. "Nancy Pelosi to Visit Taiwan Next Month amid China Tensions." *Financial Times*, July 19, 2022. https://www.ft.com/content/09669099-1565-4723-86c9-84e0ca465825.

Singleton, Craig. Interview with Michael Sobolik. "China's Overseas Military Bases." *Great Power Podcast*. November 21, 2022. https://pod

casts.apple.com/us/podcast/great-power-podcast/id15932142
89?i=1000587006442.

Stritmater, Kai. *We Have Been Harmonized: Life in China's Surveillance State.*
New York: Custom House, 2020.

Wilt, Haley Byrd. "'The Liberty of Democracy Is a Complicated Undertaking': How the Uyghur Forced Labor Prevention Act Became Law."
Dispatch. June 20, 2022. https://thedispatch.com/wp-content/uplo
ads/2022/10/How-the-Uyghur-Forced-Labor-Prevention-Act-Be
came-Law-Final-Version.pdf.

X (George F. Kennan). "The Sources of Soviet Conduct." *Foreign Affairs*,
July 1, 1947. https://www.foreignaffairs.com/russian-federation/geo
rge-kennan-sources-soviet-conduct.

Xi Jinping. *The Governance of China.* Beijing: Foreign Languages Press, 2014.

Zakaria, Fareed. "China Is Weaker Than We Thought. Will We Change Our
Policies Accordingly?" *Washington Post*, October 20, 2022. https://
www.washingtonpost.com/opinions/2022/10/20/china-weaker-
west-policies-must-adapt/.

Zarate, Juan. *Treasury's War: The Unleashing of a New Era of Financial Warfare.* New York: PublicAffairs, 2013.

Zoellick, Robert B. "Whither China: From Membership to Responsibility?" U.S. Department of State Archive, September 21, 2005. https://
2001-2009.state.gov/s/d/former/zoellick/rem/53682.htm.

INDEX

high cost of maintaining, 102–3; modern CCP version of, 83–84

Hu Jintao: effort to dispel concerns about China's rise, 50; and strategic culture of China, 40–41. 173n58; and U.S. decline, 98

Huawei, 67, 69, 74, 76, 109, 146–47

Hucker, Charles, 32

human rights violations by China: as forbidden topic in U.S.'s liberal internationalism, 129–31, 132–33; response to U.S. challenges on, as symptom of regime's insecurity, 154; as sore spot for CCP, xii; U.S. complicity in, 158. *See also* Liu Xiaobo; Uyghur genocide

imperialism: China's historical mandate to rule "all under heaven" (*Tianxia*) and, 31–32, 34, 169–70n18; China's Imperial Confucianism, 36–39, 61, 68, 100, 102, 128, 154; history of China as history of imperial expansion, 29, 37–39, 160, 172n49; return of Imperial China as goal of CCP, 19–22; stories of Chinese imperialism used by Xi to illustrate BRI, 47–48; vulnerabilities inherent in, 160; Western relinquishment of, 31–32

India: China's attempted strategic strangulation of, 60–64; present alignment with West, 60; strategic importance of, 59–60

Indian Ocean, BRI in, 59–65; in Mallaca Straits, 61; and strategic importance of India, 59–60; and strategic strangulation of India, 60–64

Indonesia, and BRI, 51

Indo-Pacific Economic Framework for Prosperity, 74

intellectual property theft by China, slow U.S. response to, 21

Internet: China's cyberattacks on U.S. government, 152–53; China's Great Cannon attacks on hostile websites, 152; China's propaganda targeting U.S., 147–48; as propaganda highway, 122; as tool for "harmonizing" world with Chinese view, 147–48

Internet censorship by China (Great Firewall): complacency of Chinese within constraints of, 148–49; pressuring of U.S. companies to support, 147, 151; thoroughness of, 129; U.S. help in building of, 146. *See also* countering Chinese Internet censorship

Iran: and BRI leverage, 56; U.S. opposition to regional hegemony, 54

Iraq, and BRI leverage, 56

Iraq War, 96–97

Italy, withdrawal from BRI, 106

Jiang Zemin, on Chinese cultural continuity, 40

Jiechi, Yang, 50–51

Kang, David, 33

Kasparov, Gary, 155–56, 161

Kennan, George, 9

Kerry, John, 71–72, 74

Kingsmith, A. T., 48–49

Kiribati, and BRI leverage, 57–58

Kissinger, Henry, 23–24, 25, 38, 110

Kritenbrink, Daniel, 120

Kuwait, and BRI leverage, 56

Kyrgyzstan, economic benefits of BRI, 55

Laos, and BRI leverage, 51

Latin America: past efforts to weaken U.S. influence in, 65; strategic value to China, 67

Latin America, BRI in, 65–68; and China's military designs, 66; China's severing of Taiwan's ties, 66; and

ABOUT THE AUTHOR

Michael Sobolik is a Senior Fellow in Indo-Pacific Studies at the American Foreign Policy Council (AFPC). Previously, he was a legislative assistant in the U.S. Senate. Sobolik's work at AFPC covers American and Chinese grand strategy, regional economic and security trends, America's alliance architecture in Asia, and human rights. He also hosts *Great Power Podcast*, a show about U.S.-China relations and great power competition. Sobolik's analysis has appeared in *Foreign Policy*, *Newsweek*, the *Dispatch*, *Jane's Defence Weekly*, *National Review*, and *RealClearDefense*, among other places.